# Balmoral

Things might be otherwise. They are in this play. The year is 1937, and the Soviet Republic of Great Britain is at the height of the purges. The royal residence of Balmoral, now a State Writers' Home, is being steadily dismantled by pilferers under the Warden's very eyes. The last ping-pong ball has just disappeared during the night, and so has one of the writers — with the capitalist press on the doorstep from St Petersburg to interview him . . .

As in *Noises Off,* appearances have to be maintained by desperate means. But this time the results are gratifying and exhilarating for all concerned . . . Originally staged as *Liberty Hall,* this revised version, now entitled *Balmoral,* was presented at the Bristol Old Vic in Spring 1987 and is published here for the first time.

**MICHAEL FRAYN** was born in 1933, in the suburbs of London. He began his career as a reporter on the *Guardian*, then wrote a column for that paper from 1959 to 1962, and for the *Observer* from 1962 to 1968. He has published five novels — *The Tin Men, The Russian Interpreter, Towards the End of the Morning, A Very Private Life,* and *Sweet Dreams,* together with a volume of philosophy, *Constructions.* He has written a number of plays for television; two original screenplays, *Clockwise* and *First and Last;* and nine plays for the stage, including *Alphabetical Order, Donkeys' Years, Clouds, Make and Break, Noises Off,* and *Benefactors.* He has translated Chekhov's last four plays, and adapted another (the play without a title) as *Wild Honey.* For some years after he left the *Observer* he continued to contribute features to the paper on foreign countries, among them Cuba, Israel, Japan, and Sweden, and he has written and presented a series of personal films for BBC Television on Berlin, Vienna, Australia, Jerusalem, and the London suburbs in which he grew up.

*by the same author*

*Plays*

Alphabetical Order
Benefactors
Clockwise (screen play)
Clouds
Donkeys' Years
Make and Break
Noises Off
The Two of Us
PLAYS: ONE (Alphabetical Order, Donkeys' Years,
  Clouds, Make and Break, Noises Off)

*Translations*

The Cherry Orchard
The Fruits of Enlightenment
The Seagull
Three Sisters
Uncle Vanya
Wild Honey

*Novels*

A Very Private Life
The Russian Interpreter
Sweet Dreams
The Tin Men
Towards the End of the Morning

*Non-fiction*

Constructions

*Journalism*

The Original Michael Frayn

MICHAEL FRAYN

# Balmoral

A METHUEN PAPERBACK

**A METHUEN MODERN PLAY**

First published in 1987 as a Methuen Paperback original
by Methuen London Ltd, 11 New Fetter Lane, London EC4P 4EE
and Methuen Inc, 29 West 35th Street, New York, NY 10001, USA

Copyright © 1987 by Michael Frayn
Set in IBM 10pt Journal by ⋎ Tek Art Limited, Croydon, Surrey
Printed and bound in Great Britain
by Richard Clay Ltd, Bungay, Suffolk

British Library Cataloguing in Publication Data

Frayn, Michael
    Balmoral. — (A Methuen modern play).
    I.  Title
    822'.914          PR6056.R3

IBSN 0 413 17180 9

CAUTION
All rights in this play are strictly reserved and application for performance
etc., should be made *by professionals* to
Fraser and Dunlop (Scripts) Ltd., 91 Regent Street, London;
and *by amateurs* to Samuel French Ltd., 52 Fitzroy Street,
London W1P 6JR. No performance may be given unless
a licence has been obtained.

An earlier version of *Balmoral,* with the same title, was first presented at the Yvonne Arnaud Theatre, Guildford, on 20 June 1978, in a production directed by Eric Thompson. A version close to the present one was first presented under the title *Liberty Hall* at the Greenwich Theatre on 24 January 1980, with the following cast:

| | |
|---|---|
| WINN | Julian Fellowes |
| DEEPING | Anthony Sharp |
| BLYTON | Rowena Cooper |
| MCNAB | Rikki Fulton |
| SKINNER | George Cole |
| TRISHA | Jill Meager |
| KOCHETOV | Oliver Cotton |

*Directed by* Alan Dossor
*Designed by* Poppy Mitchell
*Lighting by* Nick Chelton

The present version was first presented, under the title *Balmoral,* at the Bristol Old Vic on 8 May 1987, with the following cast:

| | |
|---|---|
| WINN | Mark Tandy |
| DEEPING | Anthony Pedley |
| BLYTON | Helen Ryan |
| MCNAB | Kevin Lloyd |
| SKINNER | Bernard Lloyd |
| TRISHA | Lysette Anthony |
| KOCHETOV | Kevin Wallace |

*Directed by* Leon Rubin
*Designed by* Sally Crabb
*Lighting by* John A Williams

# ACT ONE

*Balmoral. 1937.*

*A room in the castle.*

*Tartan furnishings; antlers; Landseers. A baronial fireplace, and three doors, left, right, and centre. Armchairs, a dining table, and a sideboard with breakfast things on it.     with breakfast things on it.*

*As you look at the room, however, slight discrepancies become apparent. A small electric fire burns in the great fireplace. There is an odd assortment of kitchen chairs round the dining table. A notice-board is fixed on one of the doors.*

*WINN is standing in front of the hearth, warming his backside at the little electric fire. He is 29, and is wearing plus-fours and a Fair Isle sweater. He has a newspaper under his arm and he is smiling reflectively.*

*Enter DEEPING, centre. He is 60, and is wearing an old well-cut suit, with a muffler round his neck. He has a folder of papers under his arm. He is a gentleman.*

*He stands just inside the door, looking round the room and rubbing his hands gloomily. After a moment WINN glances at him, then continues to smile to himself.*

WINN. Strange world. Strange, strange world.

*DEEPING does not rise to this. He continues to rub his hands, then turns to consult a thermometer hanging on the wall.*

Forty-eight. The temperature. In here. Freezing hard outside.

*DEEPING turns to the sideboard and helps himself without enthusiasm.*

WINN. I was out before breakfast, sniffing the air. I thought one might get a spot of shooting today. We could have a whack at the grouse. Perfect day for it.

DEEPING *sits down at the table with his kedgeree, and looks round for something.*

Paper?

*Hands* DEEPING *the newspaper he had been holding behind his back.* DEEPING *smooths it out and reads as he eats.*

Strange world, though, Warry.

DEEPING *continues to read.*

No, but seriously. Did you ever think, when you were a child, did you ever think for one moment that you would wake up one sparkling cold winter's morning in the years to come, and find the world outside all covered in white, and a tureen of steaming kedgeree on the sideboard, and realise you were a guest at Balmoral?

*No response.*

No, I believe this is going to be an awfully good year for me. When you think it's still only the fourth of January . . . I believe 1937 is going to be my year.

*Enter* BLYTON, *centre. She is 40, and is wearing several layers of cardigan. She stands just inside the door, where* DEEPING *stood before, looking round the room and gloomily rubbing her hands.*

Enid, did you ever think, when you were a little girl, did you ever so much as dream, that you might come downstairs one crackling frosty January morning, and find that you were standing in the breakfast room of a royal residence?

BLYTON *gives no sigh of having heard. She shivers.*

DEEPING (*glances up at her*). Forty-eight. To be absolutely precise.

BLYTON *gazes at him. She stops rubbing her hands.*

WINN. Alternatively, Warry, you and I could join forces and have a wallop at the poor old deer.

BLYTON *turns sharply to look at* WINN.

DEEPING (*explains*). Godfrey wants to shoot something.

WINN. Well, we are at Balmoral. That is the life here.

DEEPING (*quietly*). Do you ever want to shoot something, Enid?

WINN. No, seriously. We could get McNab to ghillie for us.

DEEPING. I sometimes want to shoot something.

WINN. No, all I'm saying is, here we are at Balmoral, and perhaps we should make a bit more effort to enjoy it.

DEEPING. Put another head up over the mantelpiece.

WINN *looks at* DEEPING, *surprised. Pause.*

BLYTON. Forty-eight?

*Pause.*

DEEPING. What?

BLYTON. Who is forty-eight?

DEEPING. *Who* is forty-eight? What do you mean, *who* is forty-eight?

BLYTON. You're not saying *I'm* forty-eight?

DEEPING. *It* is forty-eight.

BLYTON. It?

DEEPING. In here. In this room.

BLYTON (*looks slowly round the room, bewildered*). What *is* everyone talking about this morning?

*She goes to the sideboard and helps herself to kedgeree.*

DEEPING (*quietly*). *Two* more heads up over the mantelpiece.

WINN. Warry, all I'm saying is this . . .

DEEPING. Godfrey, all your immense labour is in vain.

WINN. All right — how about trying for a few rabbits?

DEEPING. I mean, Godfrey, that even if you preside over the hearth-rug in that maddening way until the seat of your trousers bursts into flame — even if you go out and slaughter all the rabbits, deer, grouse, budgerigars, and white mice in the

entire Scottish Highlands, you will not succeed in convincing
Enid and me that you are a gentleman.

*Silence.* WINN *gazes at* DEEPING. DEEPING *reads the paper.*
BLYTON *sits down and begins to shovel kedgeree into her
mouth.* WINN *looks at her, then back at* DEEPING.

WINN (*quietly*). Warry, that is a frightful thing to say. It's hurtful
and mean and it also runs directly counter to the whole spirit
of the Sixteenth Party Congress.

DEEPING. On the contrary, Godfrey. My remark was very much
in line with the spirit of the Sixteenth Party Congress. You
won't catch me like that.

WINN. Warry, why do you think we had a Revolution in Britain
in 1917?

DEEPING. Not to turn you into a gentleman, surely?

WINN. To do away with class distinction. That process is now
complete. We are at last living in a classless society. That was
spelled out in resolution after resolution at the Sixteenth Party
Congress.

*Enter* MCNAB, *right. He is 53, and is wearing a flat cap, a kilt,
and Wellington boots. He is carrying an empty champagne
bucket, with a handle improvised out of a piece of rope, and is
trailing a shovel. The champagne bucket is full of coal. No one
pays any attention to him.*

DEEPING. Exactly. There are no gentlemen, Godfrey. The
species is extinct.

WINN. That's not *my* interpretation of the Sixteenth Party
Congress.

DEEPING. What is your interpretation?

WINN. My interpretation is that we are *all* gentlemen.

*Exit* MCNAB *left.*

DEEPING. Gentlemen of the world, unite!

WINN. Marx and Engels were German. The Revolution didn't
happen in Germany. It didn't happen in France or Italy or
Russia. It happened in England. This is an English classless

society. I mean, be reasonable, Warry! Look at us. Living in luxury. Waited on hand and foot. That's why Balmoral has been made over to the people — so that the people can live like kings.

DEEPING. We're not the people. We're writers.

WINN. Writers are people, Warry! Goodness me, we're dashed important people! That's why we're given the chance of a few weeks' break in a place like Balmoral.

*Silence.*

BLYTON. What are we eating?

DEEPING. Porridge.

BLYTON. Porridge?

DEEPING. I assume.

WINN. Kedgeree.

DEEPING. This isn't kedgeree. Kedgeree is made of rice. This isn't rice.

WINN. Well, it's certainly not oats.

DEEPING. It's some kind of barley.

WINN. Porridge is made of oats.

DEEPING. It's barley gruel.

WINN. Barley kedgeree.

BLYTON. It's got turnips in.

WINN. Barley and turnip kedgeree.

DEEPING. Or turnip soup with barley.

*Enter* MCNAB, *left. He is carrying the champagne bucket and trailing the shovel, as before, but the bucket is now empty, and he is wearing a green baize apron under his jacket and over his kilt. He heads towards the righthand door.*

WINN. Why don't we ask McNab? John, what are these good people eating?

MCNAB. Kedgeree.

WINN. Kedgeree. And what sort of kedgeree?

MCNAB. Barley and turnip kedgeree.

WINN. Thank you, John.

DEEPING. McNab, what leads you to suppose that this is kedgeree?

MCNAB. I cooked it.

DEEPING. But, McNab, why do you assume the result is called *kedgeree*?

MCNAB. Because it's Wednesday.

DEEPING. Thank you, McNab.

WINN. Thank you, John.

*Exit* MCNAB, *right.*

All I'm saying is we ought not to sit on our backsides and work all the time.

DEEPING. Walpole's still not down. He seems to have given up breakfast entirely these days. I wonder why.

WINN. All right, we all want to work.

DEEPING. He scarcely leaves his room from one day's end to the next.

WINN. *I* want to work. I *do* work. I did two hours work in here before breakfast.

DEEPING. He has a warm room, of course.

WINN. All I'm saying is that if they send you off to spend the winter season in a royal residence, and then you turn round and make no effort at all to enjoy it, then it does seem to me just a shade ungrateful, if not downright counter to the whole spirit of the Sixteenth Party Congress.

DEEPING. Hugh Walpole has the kitchen flue running through the wall of his bedroom. But then Hugh Walpole has a cousin running through the upper echelons of the Party.

*Silence.*

BLYTON. My hot water bottle has gone.

DEEPING. Everything goes in this place.

WINN. Only if it's left around.

BLYTON. I can't sleep without a hot water bottle.

DEEPING. Half the lead off the roof has gone.

WINN. Let's not exaggerate, Warry. There's a lot still there.

DEEPING. All the bath plugs have gone.

BLYTON. I can't work without a hot water bottle.

DEEPING. The whole castle is going bit by bit.

WINN. You'll have to work in here, like the rest of us.

DEEPING. Apart from Hugh.

BLYTON. I can't work in the same room as other people.

WINN. It's only Warry and me.

DEEPING. Think what it's going to be like in the summer when this place is full. Imagine twenty or thirty writers living and working in here.

WINN. All complaining about the food.

DEEPING. All saying they can't work in the same room as other people.

BLYTON. I shall be dead before the summer.

*Enter* MCNAB, *right, with the champagne bucket and the shovel. But the bucket is now full of coal, and he is no longer wearing the green baize apron. He heads towards the lefthand door.*

(*to* MCNAB.) Have you seen a hot water bottle anywhere?

MCNAB. No.

WINN. John, is there a gun about the place?

MCNAB. No.

WINN. How about a pair of skates?

MCNAB. No.

DEEPING. Were you ever savagely punished, McNab, for talking in school?

MCNAB. No.

*Exit* MCNAB.

WINN. He has a lot to contend with, though. He has all the cooking to do, for a start.

DEEPING. I shouldn't call that cooking.

WINN. Remember he has all the cleaning, as well. All the washing. All the gardening.

DEEPING. All the stealing.

WINN. All the maintenance to the castle.

DEEPING. Fancy trying to run a place this size with one under-coachman!

WINN. He's not an under-coachman.

DEEPING. Before the Revolution he was an under-coachman.

WINN. Well, now he's a butler.

DEEPING. You can't seriously think of him as a butler!

WINN. Give him time. People grow to fill their jobs. Everyone knows that.

DEEPING. What about Skinner?

WINN. The Warden? The Warden is exactly the kind of case I'm talking about . . .

*Enter* SKINNER, *centre. He is a man of about fifty, and is wearing a neat dark suit, with a dark shirt and tie. He is holding a selection of ledgers.*

DEEPING. Good morning, Skinner.

WINN. Hello, Warden!

DEEPING. We were just talking about you.

SKINNER *does not respond. He slaps the ledgers down, and runs a sombrely assessing eye over the room.*

WINN. Anything I can do, Warden . . .? Are you looking for something?

SKINNER *crosses to the sideboard and picks up a half-empty milk bottle.*

Tea? Can I pour you a cup of tea, Warden?

*Enter* MCNAB, *left, with the champagne bucket. He is wearing the green baize apron, but is trailing a mop instead of the shovel, and the bucket is full of water.* SKINNER *watches the bucket narrowly as* MCNAB *crosses to the righthand door.*

SKINNER. Fetching more coal, McNab?

MCNAB. Washing down the hall.

SKINNER. With a champagne bucket?

MCNAB. With the coal bucket.

SKINNER. That's a champagne bucket.

MCNAB. Only bucket left.

SKINNER. All right.

MCNAB. All right?

SKINNER. All right.

*Exit* MCNAB, *right. Exit* SKINNER, *centre holding the milk bottle.*

DEEPING. You were saying?

WINN. I was saying the Warden is exactly the kind of case I'm talking about. Do you know what he was before the Revolution?

DEEPING. Cashier at the Clapham Junction Home and Colonial.

WINN. Yes, and within twelve years he was running the entire British tram-building industry.

DEEPING. And now he's sunk to being Warden of a state writers' home.

WINN. That's nothing to sneer at.

DEEPING. But he can't do it, can he. It's beyond him! They'll be coming for him one of these days. A ring at the doorbell at six o'clock in the morning. Then we'll come down to breakfast and — no Skinner!

WINN. Honestly, Warry! That's not the kind of thing to joke about.

DEEPING. What's he doing with that milk?

*Enter* SKINNER, *right, with the milk bottle. The milk has been emptied out, and a single bare twig put in its place. He gazes round the room, trying to see where it would create most effect.*

WINN. Oh, look, we've got a twig this morning! That'll brighten the place up.

SKINNER *tries the milk bottle in various locations. He stands back and sombrely assesses the effect.*

DEEPING. Is it the inspection today, then, Skinner?

WINN. How can he know whether it's today or not? It's going to be a surprise inspection. That's the whole point.

DEEPING. He may have had a tip-off.

WINN. Is it today, Warden?

DEEPING. They've done the painters and graphic artists at Sandringham. I had a letter from Spencer.

WINN. They've done the opera people at Holyrood. They arrested the catering manager and two baritones.

DEEPING. It'll be Skinner's turn sooner or later.

WINN. Anyway, the twig's nice.

*Having settled the position of the twig,* SKINNER *sits down and opens his ledgers.*

SKINNER. Right, let's get this meeting out of the way.

DEEPING. Meeting? What meeting?

SKINNER. Don't you ever look at the timetable?

WINN. Oh, the union meeting!

SKINNER. Right, minutes of the last meeting?

WINN. I move they be taken as read.

SKINNER. Seconded?

WINN (*prompting*). Warry?

DEEPING *shrugs and raises his arm.*

SKINNER (*signs the minutes*). Treasurer's report?

WINN. I move the report be received.

SKINNER. Seconded?

DEEPING. Your turn, Enid.

BLYTON (*suddenly becoming conscious of the world*). What?

WINN. Treasurer's report. We need a seconder.

BLYTON. What is everyone talking about?

DEEPING. Just raise your arm, Enid.

  *She raises her arm blankly.*

SKINNER. Three. This branch will send a delegation to the
  Smash Tsarism rally in Edinburgh on Sunday, with the branch
  banner. Proposed?

WINN (*gently*). Warry . . .

  DEEPING *raises his arm.*

SKINNER. Seconded?

WINN. Enid . . .

  BLYTON *raises her arm.*

SKINNER. Four. This branch warmly welcomes the regional
  committee's call for increased production and a higher level of
  labour enthusiasm . . .

  *Enter* MCNAB, *right, with the champagne bucket, empty, the
  mop, and no baize apron. He crosses towards the left-hand
  door.*

  . . . and pledges an increase of six hours a week in voluntary
  unpaid overtime. Proposed?

WINN. Enid . . .

  BLYTON *raises her arm.*

SKINNER. Seconded?

  WINN *raises his arm.*

  Five. Someone has stolen the ping-pong ball.

WINN. Oh my God.

DEEPING. What next?

MCNAB. The bellrope's gone.

*Exit* MCNAB, *left.*

SKINNER. I sit in my office in there working on the books. Keeping the books straight. I can't watch the ping-pong ball, the bellrope, the frying-pan, the billiard cue . . .

DEEPING (*to* WINN). We're going to be losing our half-holiday.

WINN. Warry, this is serious.

SKINNER. Look, any inspectors coming here, they're going to find these books in apple-pie order. If the books say I have one billiard-cue and four writers, then by heaven . . . Just a moment. Where's Deeping?

WINN (*indicating*). Here.

SKINNER. Then where's Blyton?

WINN. Here. It's Walpole, Warden. He never came down to breakfast.

SKINNER. Six. This branch condemns the brutal suppression of the strikes by motor industry workers in St. Petersburg, and calls upon the Russian Imperial Government to recognise trade union freedom.

*Enter* MCNAB, *left, without mop or shovel, but wearing the green baize apron and carrying the champagne bucket. It is now full of kitchen swill.*

Proposed?

WINN *raises his arm.*

Seconded?

DEEPING *raises his arm.*

Any other business? No other business. Are you building a swimming pool out there, McNab?

MCNAB *stops on his way towards the righthand door.*

*Another* bucket of water?

MCNAB. Bucket of swill.

SKINNER. You're washing the floor with swill?

MCNAB. Feeding the pigs.

SKINNER. Oh, yes, you're feeding the pigs. With a bucket of swill. And who knows what sins are concealed in a bucket of swill?

*He gets up and goes over to* MCNAB.

You see now why I've nailed up the back door? So that everything comes past me, McNab. Buckets of water, buckets of swill — they all pass before my beady eye. You're not the first person in the world to have tried putting it across on me, McNab. During my years in industry I had many thousands of men working under my management, and I can tell you — you don't know what thieving is. I have seen entire factories dismantled virtually in front of my eyes. I have seen complete grand hotels get up and walk out through the service entrance. I have seen a crack express leave Manchester Victoria complete with dining-car, Pullmans, and Pullman waiters, and turn up one week later at Wolverhampton High Level stripped to the bogies. So don't expect me to be impressed because you stole the doorbell last Thursday. Don't expect me to be amazed because the bell-rope's gone now.

MCNAB. Went ten times or more.

SKINNER. Never mind the bell rope. I want to see what you've got in that bucket.

MCNAB. In the bucket? Swill.

SKINNER. Show me, McNab.

MCNAB. Show you?

SKINNER. Show me.

MCNAB *tips the swill out on the floor.* SKINNER *gazes at it unseeingly. Another thought has struck him.*

Went ten times?

MCNAB. What?

SKINNER. The bellrope. How it could go ten times?

MCNAB. Because this fellow on the doorstep keeps pulling it! I saw him with my own eyes! Up and down, up and down it goes! Then this fellow looks through the letter box at me and he starts pulling it again.

SKINNER. What fellow looked through the letter box?

MCNAB. This fellow in the peaked cap.

SKINNER (*awestruck*). Peaked cap?

MCNAB. Driver of the car.

SKINNER. There's a car outside! An official car? And you've left them standing in the snow?

MCNAB. 'Let no one in!' Your words, Mr Skinner. No one to come in without the say-so from yourself.

SKINNER. Let them in.

MCNAB. You want them in?

SKINNER. Not you. (*To* WINN.) You.

WINN (*goes to the righthand door, in a flutter*). Oh dear. This is the inspector, is it?

SKINNER. Come back, come back. I'll go. You get this place straight. Breakfast! Breakfast! Get it out of here!

WINN *goes to the sideboard and begins clearing up the remains of breakfast.* MCNAB *stands where he was left, watching the activity all around.*

(*to* BLYTON *and* DEEPING.) You two — don't stand about like a bread queue. Get down to some work.

DEEPING. What about the ping-pong ball?

SKINNER. Leave all the thinking to me. You just get on with the writing.

DEEPING *and* BLYTON *prepare to write.*

No, go and fetch the paraffin stove out of my office.

*They rise.*

SKINNER (*to* BLYTON). Sit down!

*Exit* DEEPING, *centre.* WINN *takes the plates towards the lefthand door, leaving the tureen of kedgeree behind on the sideboard.*

WINN. In the kitchen?

SKINNER (*indicates the kedgeree*). The other thing! Take the other thing! (*To* BLYTON.) Pen open! This is a writers' home! *Somebody* be writing!

WINN. The kedgeree?

SKINNER. *That* stuff! Get it out of here! Put it in the kitchen!

WINN *returns to the sideboard, puts down his armful of plates, picks up the kedgeree, and heads back towards the lefthand door.* SKINNER *meanwhile is discovering a suspiciously clean patch on the wallpaper.*

Antlers! A set of antlers missing! (*To* WINN.) Plates!

WINN *returns to the sideboard and struggles to hold both plates and tureen of kedgeree.*

(*To* BLYTON.) Antlers! Another set of antlers!

BLYTON *gets up and begins to search hopelessly for some extra antlers.*

*Enter* DEEPING, *centre, carrying a paraffin stove.*

(*To* DEEPING.) Antlers! Antlers!

DEEPING. Antlers?

*He puts down the paraffin stove, and takes down one of the other sets of antlers.*

SKINNER (*to* BLYTON). You — start writing!

BLYTON *goes back to the table.*

(*To* MCNAB.) What do you think *you're* doing? (*Indicates the swill on the floor.*) Put it back!

DEEPING (*holding the antlers*). Put it back?

SKINNER (*to* MCNAB). Put it back!

MCNAB *begins to pick up handfuls of swill and put them back in the bucket.* DEEPING *starts to put the antlers back on the wall.*

(*To* DEEPING.) Not there! There!

DEEPING *takes the antlers across to the clean patch.* MCNAB *takes the directions as applying to the swill, and carries a handfull of it across the room.* WINN *struggles towards the lefthand door, beginning to drop his load of breakfast things.*

(*To* WINN.) Oh, for heaven's sake! Put it back where you found it!

DEEPING *takes the antlers back to where he found them.* MCNAB *takes the swill back to where it was.*

(*To* DEEPING.) Not you! Him!

WINN *struggles to pick up the items he has dropped.* MCNAB, *now totally confused, holds the dripping handful of swill over anything except the bucket.*

(*To* WINN.) Leave it! Sit down!

MCNAB *sits down, still holding the swill.*

(*To* DEEPING.) You — get the books out of my office!

DEEPING (*runs to the centre door, still holding the antlers, then stops*). What books?

SKINNER. 'What books?' Can't you people do *anything*? Sit down! (*To* MCNAB.) Stand up! (*To* WINN.) Let them in!

WINN. Let them in?

SKINNER. Let them in!

WINN *hurriedly dumps the kedgeree and the rest of the breakfast things on the nearest armchair, and goes out, right.*

(*To* DEEPING *and* BLYTON.) Write! Write!

(*To* MCNAB.) Wipe that swill off the floor!

*Exit* SKINNER, *centre.*

DEEPING *and* BLYTON *bend over their work* — DEEPING *still encumbered by the antlers.*

MCNAB *dumps his handful of swill in the bucket. Then he rips a piece of loose tartan wallpaper off the wall, gets down on his hands and knees, and begins to wipe the floor.*

DEEPING (*quietly*). Hide your eyes, Enid.

BLYTON. What?

DEEPING. Murder is going to be done at this inspection. Friend Skinner is going to be minced fine and fried in batter. Trussed and stuffed and roasted.

MCNAB. We're all in the same pan. If they roast the goose they'll roast the potatoes, too.

*Enter* TRISHA *and* KOCHETOV, *right, followed by* WINN, TRISHA *is 20, and is wearing a warm overcoat and a woolly hat.* KOCHETOV *is 26, and is wearing an expensive winter overcoat trimmed with fur. His is Russian, but speaks perfect English, with only a slight Russian intonation. His surname is stressed on the first syllable — KAWCHETOV.*

DEEPING *and* BLYTON *get to their feet.*

TRISHA. Hello. Mr Skinner?

DEEPING. No, no.

WINN. This is Mr Deeping. Mr Skinner will be here in one moment.

*The three writers gaze at* KOCHETOV *and* TRISHA, *overawed;* MCNAB *wipes the floor and listens.*

KOCHETOV (*entirely at his ease*). Charming room.

WINN. Yes.

DEEPING. Yes.

KOCHETOV. You must tell me where you get your tartan linoleum. Three writers — and you all work happily together in the same room?

WINN.  
DEEPING.  } Yes.  
BLYTON.

KOCHETOV. The perfect community. Please — write, write. write!

WINN. Oh.

DEEPING. Well.

BLYTON. Thank you.

    WINN, DEEPING *and* BLYTON *sit down simultaneously.*

KOCHETOV. I've seen people writing with a quill. I've never seen anyone writing with antlers before.

DEEPING. Oh yes. (*He puts the antlers aside.*) We were rearranging the room.

KOCHETOV. I have a feeling that we have taken you somewhat by surprise.

DEEPING. Not at all.

WINN. Yes, entirely.

TRISHA. I'm sorry, I should explain — this is Mr Kochetov.

    WINN, DEEPING *and* BLYTON *rise, in unison.*

KOCHETOV. Please, please.

    *They sit, in unison.*

    Perfect.

TRISHA. Mr Kochetov is a Russian journalist.

KOCHETOV. The capitalist press, I'm afraid. Vulgar, sensational, and appallingly readable. And this is my mistress.

TRISHA (*deeply embarrassed*). Mr Kochetov, please!

KOCHETOV. My future mistress. Yes? My mistress-to-be.

TRISHA. Honestly . . . ! Mr Kochetov is a terrible tease.

KOCHETOV. Well, my love, it's impossible. You're like a shiny new rosy-cheeked apple. I can't help wanting to sink my teeth into you.

TRISHA. I'm Mr Kochetov's guide from the Board of Trade.

KOCHETOV. Her job is to stop me seeing all the things I'm not supposed to see.

TRISHA. That's not true! You can see anything you like! I've told you before — freedom of the press is guaranteed under the constitution. I'm just here to help you.

WINN. Just a moment. This gentleman is a *journalist?*

TRISHA. Yes, and he's a complete cynic.

WINN. A *Russian* journalist?

KOCHETOV. Oh, but I had a most excellent English governess.

TRISHA. He tells everyone we meet about his English governess.

KOCHETOV. No, but she prepared me very well for understanding this country, you see, because she was entirely held together by safety pins. So whenever I look at something here and I can't believe my eyes, I simply remember my old governess. Of course, I think. Safety pins! It's all held together by safety pins! This, I need hardly say, will be the first paragraph of my article.

WINN. But — sorry — you're not the inspector?

KOCHETOV. Inspector? (*To* TRISHA.) Am I the inspector?

TRISHA. I don't know anything about inspectors. Mr Kochetov is simply here to interview Hugh Walpole for the Russian newspapers.

WINN. Interview . . . ?

KOCHETOV. May we sit down?

WINN. Yes. Yes.

*Without looking he indicates the chair where he put the breakfast things.*

Newspapers? Russian newspapers?

*He realises that* KOCHETOV *is gazing at the breakfast things.*

Oh, I'm so sorry!

WINN *picks up the tureen of kedgeree and hands it to* MCNAB, *who is standing waiting with the bucket of swill beside him, then picks up the rest of the breakfast things.*

*Enter* SKINNER, *centre with a stack of ledgers.*

SKINNER. I do apologise! But I know you'll want to look at the books before you do anything else. Oh dear. Has no one even taken your coats? Writers, I'm afraid! Heads in the clouds. Feet not quite on the ground. How do you do?

TRISHA. This is Mr Kochetov.

KOCHETOV. How do you do?

SKINNER. Skinner, Skinner.

WINN (*urgently, still holding the breakfast things*). Warden . . .

SKINNER (*to* WINN). I don't want them! (*To* KOCHETOV.)
    May I . . .?

*He helps* KOCHETOV *off with his coat, cunningly turning him
away from* WINN *and the breakfast things as he does so, which
brings him instead face to face with* MCNAB *and the tureen of
kedgeree.*

WINN. Mr Kochetov is a journalist. A Russian journalist.

SKINNER (*to* WINN). Just get that stuff out of here, will you?
    (*To* KOCHETOV.) We do try to keep a fairly informal
    atmosphere in here . . .

*He realises that* KOCHETOV *is gazing with interest at the
kedgeree.*

That is pigswill. It has been duly certified as unfit for human
consumption.

MCNAB. This is kedgeree. (*He bends and picks up the bucket of
swill.*)

SKINNER. And this is kedgeree. We like to keep a tureen of
    kedgeree to hand in case of unexpected guests.

MCNAB. This is pigswill.

SKINNER. This is pigswill. Have you been offered some . . . ? *This*
    is pigswill?

*He looks from swill to kedgeree in confusion.*

MCNAB. You want to see it?

*He offers to tip the swill out on the floor again.*

SKINNER. No, thank you! Just put it back on the sideboard,
    McNab.

MCNAB. The swill?

SKINNER. The kedgeree, the kedgeree. (*To* KOCHETOV.) Now,

where do you want to work? I expect you'd prefer to shut yourself away in my office.

*He steers* KOCHETOV *firmly towards the centre door.*

TRISHA. I think all Mr Kochetov really wants to do is to sit down quietly somewhere and have a little chat with Mr Walpole.

SKINNER. Of course. If he wants to talk privately, I think he'd find my office more convenient . . . Mr Walpole?

WINN. I tried to tell you.

TRISHA. I can't believe I'm going to meet him at last! I've read everything he's written! I've read *Rogue Herries* five times! People are always talking about what a refined sensibility Henry James has. But I think Hugh Walpole is much more refined!

KOCHETOV. The only thing one can say about her literary judgement is that she has perfect eyebrows.

TRISHA (*to* SKINNER). They did tell you about the interview?

SKINNER. Interview?

WINN. You wouldn't listen.

TRISHA. Mr Kochetov is Russian. He's interviewing Hugh Walpole for the Russian newspapers.

KOCHETOV. They adore him in Russia. Or so Trisha tells me.

TRISHA. Well, *you* wouldn't know! All you're interested in is motor-cars and girls!

KOCHETOV. I know nothing, you see. She has to tell me everything.

SKINNER. You mean you don't want to go through the books?

TRISHA. Not now. I've read all his books!

KOCHETOV. Even I have read one of them.

TRISHA. No, you haven't.

KOCHETOV. On the train.

TRISHA. Half of one.

SKINNER. You want to interview Mr Walpole? All right. (*To* MCNAB.) Fetch Mr Walpole.

MCNAB. He's not there.

SKINNER. What do you mean he's not there?

MCNAB. He's gone.

SKINNER. Gone?

MCNAB. He went out of here this morning.

SKINNER. No one's left the house!

MCNAB. Before you were up.

WINN. I've been up since six!

MCNAB. He went before six.

*Pause.*

WINN. Before six?

BLYTON. Went?

DEEPING. Walpole?

WINN, DEEPING *and* BLYTON *stare at* MCNAB. MCNAB *picks up the bucket of swill and crosses to the righthand door.*

MCNAB. You want me to tell you where he went?

WINN (*hurriedly*). No, thank you, McNab.

*Exit* MCNAB, *right.*

SKINNER (*to* WINN, *realising*). You mean . . .?

WINN. Yes!

SKINNER. You don't mean . . .?

DEEPING (*sombrely*). I think we do.

*Pause.*

TRISHA. I don't understand.

WINN. Telegram. I've just remembered. He had a telegram.

DEEPING. Of course! He had a telegram!

SKINNER (*reinforcing them as best he can*). Telegram.

WINN. Father ill.

BLYTON. Mother dying.

DEEPING. Come at once.

SKINNER. In the middle of the night.

WINN. I'd forgotten that.

DEEPING. We'd all forgotten.

SKINNER. It went out of our heads.

BLYTON. Now we've remembered.

SKINNER. It's come back to us.

TRISHA. What's happening? I don't understand! What's going on?

WINN. Nothing.

SKINNER. Nothing!

KOCHETOV. Look at her.

TRISHA (*to* SKINNER). What are you trying to hide from me?

KOCHETOV. Trisha! My dear Trisha! Let me tell you something. You are the perfect Government guide. (*To the others.*) Everything she tells me I believe! The only trouble is, I think she believes it *herself.*

TRISHA. What have I said wrong now?

KOCHETOV. Well, my darling, it's only too clear what has happened to poor old Hugh Walpole. They have taken him out and shot him.

TRISHA. Mr Kochetov, please don't say things like that.

KOCHETOV (*to the others*). Am I right?

WINN. Certainly not.

SKINNER. Absolutely not.

DEEPING. Where did you get such an idea from?

SKINNER. Ridiculous idea.

BLYTON. We don't know what you're talking about.

SKINNER. Yes, what are you talking about?

KOCHETOV (*to* TRISHA). You see? They've shot him. This is going to make the most wonderful article!

TRISHA. I know you only do it to tease me.

KOCHETOV. Yes, because you're so beautiful when you're angry. Your cheeks glow, your eyes flash . . .

TRISHA. No one in this country is taken outside and shot.

KOCHETOV. You mean they don't even trouble to take them outside now?

TRISHA. I've already explained to you, several times — the rights of the individual here are most strictly safeguarded.

KOCHETOV. Look at her! Look at her! I'm so good for her complexion! But, Trisha, my darling, have a care. Because if you go on asking where Mr Walpole is they will take *you* outside and shoot you, and that would ruin your looks.

TRISHA (*to* SKINNER). Is there a telephone here?

SKINNER. In my office.

TRISHA. I shall place a trunk call through to London direct and get all this sorted out. (*To* KOCHETOV.) Hugh Walpole has not been shot, and I am going to find him for you if I have to go to John O'Groats to do it. And I do *not* believe everything I say! I mean, I don't say everything I believe. I mean . . . Oh! Where am I going?

SKINNER. Through here. Straight across the corridor. I shall have to charge you for the call, of course, to keep my books straight.

*Exit* TRISHA, *centre*.

KOCHETOV. Her first job since she left school. And everywhere we go, it's a disaster. We have lunch at the Ritz — and we wait one hour and forty minutes to be served. We visit a new sanatorium — and the doorhandle comes off in her hand. Now she takes me to see her favourite writer, and he has just disappeared in the middle of the night. Poor Trisha!

WINN. Yes, but look on the positive side. Think of all the writers who *haven't* disappeared in the middle of the night! Why don't you interview Warwick Deeping instead? His novels are very widely read in this country.

DEEPING. Or Godfrey Winn, for that matter. An astonishingly adaptable writer.

WINN. Yes, or Enid Blyton.

DEEPING. Enid is quite well known for her curiously obscure erotic verse.

WINN. They all come to Balmoral, you know! H.G. Wells — Bernard Shaw. You never know who's going to walk through that door next.

*Enter* MCNAB, *right. He is carrying the mop and the champagne bucket, empty, but not wearing the apron. He crosses towards the lefthand door.* KOCHETOV *watches him.*

Well, they tend to come more in summer, people like Wells and Shaw. This is really a summer place, of course. You might look out of this window and see footmen hurrying across the lawn with trays of ices. You might see the band of the Coldstream Guards playing on the terrace. In summer.

MCNAB (*to* SKINNER, *on the point of going out left*). All right?

SKINNER. Yes, yes, yes . . . Where's your apron? I don't know what our visitor must be thinking. (*To* KOCHETOV.) The butler — and half the time he comes waltzing through here without his green baize apron!

*Exit* MCNAB *left.*

KOCHETOV. I must find my little girl guide. You know, I think this is going to be really rather a prize-winning article. I can't help wondering, though, what will happen to all the people who feature in it. (*Laughs.*) Will they arrest the director of the sanatorium, do you suppose? Will they shoot the manager of the Ritz? Am I leaving a trail of official corpses all the way across England? A terrible responsibility we journalists bear!

*Exit* KOCHETOV, *centre.*

DEEPING. Poor old Walpole.

WINN. I suppose it might be only ten years. He could be out again by 1947.

DEEPING. Funny they should arrest *him.*

WINN. Yes — so much for his cousin in high places.

DEEPING. After all we've endured about his influence in certain quarters.

SKINNER. I think we're in the clear, though, aren't we?

DEEPING. In the clear? In the newspapers — that's where you're going to be!

SKINNER (*uneasily*). In the newspapers?

DEEPING. In this Russian fellow's article!

WINN. It won't just be the Warden. We're all going to be in it.

DEEPING. Up to our necks. Then we're *all* going to wake up one morning and find we left during the night.

SKINNER. So what are we going to do?

DEEPING. Enid's keeping very quiet.

WINN. Have you got some ideas, Enid?

BLYTON. The room's vacant, then?

WINN. The room? What room?

BLYTON. Hugh Walpole's room. The room with the kitchen flue running through it. The warm room.

SKINNER. Never mind about the room. Let's keep our minds on one thing at a time.

WINN *moves quietly and inconspicuously towards the centre door.*

Now, we're all in this together . . . Where are you off to?

WINN. Would you excuse me? I've just got to slip upstairs.

DEEPING. Oh, no, you don't! (*To* SKINNER.) Tell him he can't do that!

BLYTON (*to* SKINNER). Stop him! Stop them both!

SKINNER. What?

BLYTON. It was my idea!

DEEPING. I am the senior writer present!

WINN. And I'm first in the queue!

*Exit* WINN, *centre* DEEPING *and* BLYTON *fight to be next through the door.*

BLYTON. Excuse me!

DEEPING. I beg your pardon!

BLYTON. Appalling manners!

DEEPING. Disgusting display!

*Exit* DEEPING, *centre.*

BLYTON (*to* SKINNER). It's not fair! It's not fair!

SKINNER. What is all this?

BLYTON. They're going to steal the room!

*Exit* BLYTON, *centre.*

SKINNER (*goes to follow them*). Room? What room? Never mind about the room!

*Enter* WALPOLE, *right. He is 53, and is wearing thick spectacles, and overcoat, hat, and galoshes. He is in a considerable state of ill humour. He bears some passing resemblance to* MCNAB, *possibly because he is played by the same actor.*

WALPOLE. It really is too bad!

SKINNER (*whirls round*). And don't *you* try slipping past, McNab, because I have eyes in the back of my . . . Walpole!

WALPOLE. I intend to lodge a formal complaint with the authorities!

SKINNER. You're here!

WALPOLE. You may well look surprised! I could have been killed out there!

SKINNER. But . . . you *escaped?*

WALPOLE. Escaped? I escaped *death,* if that's what you mean.

*Enter* BLYTON, *centre.*

BLYTON (*to* SKINNER). He's throwing everything out of the

room into the corridor! Hair-brushes, suits, dirty socks . . .
(*Sees* WALPOLE.) Oh, my God!

WALPOLE. Yes! Every bone in my body is jarred. I am bruised
from here to here. I may well have concussion.

*Enter* DEEPING, *centre*.

DEEPING (*to* SKINNER). He's thrown the man's mother out into
the corridor now! A photograph in a silver frame, and he's
tossed it aside like so much . . . Walpole!

BLYTON. They broke his bones! They hit him over the head!

WALPOLE. And how long I lay in the snow out there I know
not. I am dangerously chilled.

*Enter* WINN, *centre*.

WINN. I've put my cabin trunk in the room and locked the door.
So I hope there'll be no more . . . Hugh!

BLYTON. They beat him black and blue!

DEEPING. They left him in the snow!

WALPOLE. My muffler is sodden. I have melted snow running
down my neck.

WINN. But . . . they let you go?

WALPOLE. What?

WINN. They arrested you — and then they let you go again?

WALPOLE. Arrested me? What in heaven's name are you talking
about?

DEEPING. Hold on a moment. You mean . . . you *weren't*
arrested?

WALPOLE. Arrested? Me? *I'm* not the one who should be
arrested! I have been standing in a queue outside the Co-op
since six o'clock this morning. There was a rumour, according
to McNab, that a delivery of ladies' winter underwear was
expected. When it arrived, of course, it turned out to be usual
itchy rubbish they sell for men. I get back here, frozen to the
marrow, and find that certain people have turned the front
doorstep into a skating-rink!

WINN. And you slipped?

WALPOLE. I may have fractured my skull! The same story every morning since the chain disappeared from the upstairs loo. There's a perfectly good earth closet at the back of the piggeries. But, oh no — not for some people! Not in the middle of the night! Not when it's below freezing! What does it matter? they think. Anything goes these days! So it's up with the bedroom window, and devil take the hindermost! But if you can't learn self-control, you might at least look to see what's below!

*Exit* WALPOLE, *centre.*

DEEPING. Oh, dear.

SKINNER. Is he trying to tell us he *wasn't* arrested?

WINN. I'm afraid we all rather jumped to conclusions.

SKINNER (*brooding*). McNab, that was. McNab again.

DEEPING. Never mind about McNab.

SKINNER. Yes, but where does it leave us? That Russian thinks Walpole's been shot!

WINN. But, Warden, it's all right! Because now he can see he hasn't been!

SKINNER. That girl's out there telling London he's disappeared!

WINN. But, Warden, now she can see he hasn't disappeared!

SKINNER. You mean . . . tell them they can interview him?

DEEPING. Slowly, as if through treacle, the penny drops.

SKINNER. You mean . . . say McNab said . . .?

WINN. Say anything!

DEEPING. He's here now. That's all that matters.

SKINNER. There's a catch in this somewhere.

*Exit* SKINNER *centre.*

WINN. I see what you mean about Skinner. He does rather go to pieces under pressure.

BLYTON. It'll be coming through that door, won't it. Any moment now.

WINN. What will?

BLYTON. The catch. Well, what sort of interview do you think Hugh is going to give when you've finished explaining to him?

WINN. Explaining to him? Explaining what to him?

*Enter* WALPOLE *centre holding a framed photograph.*

WALPOLE. My mother!

WINN. What?

WALPOLE. My mother! Lying in the corridor! Suits! Collars! Tooth powder! Everywhere!

WINN. Oh my God. The room.

WALPOLE. You, is it, Winn? Have you gone quite insane?

WINN. Hugh, listen. This is going to sound rather bad, but the thing is, I thought . . . Well, we *all* thought . . . I mean, Enid suggested . . . I'll put it back.

*Exit* WINN, *centre.*

WALPOLE. The man has gone berserk! He must be locked up!

BLYTON. Have you looked *inside* the room yet?

WALPOLE. Inside the room?

DEEPING. Enid, don't work him up!

BLYTON. You'll find a cabin trunk in there.

WALPOLE. A cabin trunk? I don't *possess* a cabin trunk!

BLYTON. Godfrey Winn possesses a cabin trunk.

WALPOLE. But this is naked violation!

*Exit* WALPOLE, *centre.*

DEEPING. You shouldn't have done that, Enid. He's going to go his very bright red colour.

BLYTON (*sombrely*). He won't be able to breathe. He won't be able to speak.

DEEPING. He's already the colour of his precious ladies' underwear.

*Enter* SKINNER *and* KOCHETOV, *centre.*

KOCHETOV (*to* SKINNER). Privacy?

SKINNER (*genial*). We do try to protect it here.

KOCHETOV. By saying people have disappeared during the night?

SKINNER. We were pulling your leg.

KOCHETOV. And I may interview him?

SKINNER. Of course.

KOCHETOV *looks at* BLYTON.

BLYTON (*shrugs*). Why not? It's a free country.

DEEPING. I'll fetch him in, shall I?

*Exit* DEEPING, *centre.*

KOCHETOV. Heartbreaking. It was going to be such a wonderful article.

SKINNER. I'm sorry to disappoint you.

KOCHETOV. Oh well. It will make Trisha happy. And if Trisha is happy, perhaps our journey back to London will be fruitful.

*Exit* KOCHETOV, *centre.*

SKINNER (*genial*). The night train from Aberdeen! That's the life, Blyton! I think if I could choose where I wanted to live I should make my home in a first-class sleeper. All yesterday's troubles miles behind, all tomorrow's miles ahead. Just a little warm room speeding through the night. Nothing in the whole wide world but the bedside light shining on the papers in your despatch box. And in the morning, a limousine waiting — everyone smiling, everyone pleased to see you. Well, it will come again, Blyton, it will come again.

*Enter* MCNAB, *left, wearing an apron and carrying the mop and champagne bucket of swill. He crosses slowly to the righthand door behind* SKINNER's *back.*

I'm not as big a fool as some of you think. I don't say much. I keep quiet. I bide my time. I wait until I can reach out and catch the wrongdoer red-handed, in the very act of removing yet another champagne bucket. Don't rush away, McNab. Let me tell you some sad news. That is the oldest trick in the business. Wheelbarrow loads of old straw. They keep searching the straw. And what are you stealing? You're stealing wheelbarrows. I've seen it before, McNab — I've seen it all before. You thought; the poor fool's going to keep checking the contents of the bucket. I thought; how much rope shall I give him to hang himself? Do you know what I did this morning, McNab? I stuck a tuppeny stamp on the bottom of the bucket. So that when I pick up *this* bucket . . .

*Lifts the bucket above his head.*

SKINNER. . . . and discover to my surprise there is *no* tuppeny stamp on the bottom, then I have proof positive . . .

*Looks at the bottom of the bucket. Silence. Then he hands the bucket back to MCNAB.*

The pigs?

MCNAB. The pigs.

SKINNER. Off you go, then, McNab.

*Exit MCNAB, right.*

SKINNER *stands lost in thought.*

He's stealing something, though. I know that. It couldn't be tuppenny stamps?

*Enter WINN, centre, in a great state of agitation.*

WINN. Warden! Warden! Hugh Walpole is running amok! I *tried* to explain. I *said* I'd move everything out. But as soon as he saw my stuff he just lost control. He's throwing everything out into the corridor! There's four hundred pages of manuscript scattered all over the main stairs!

SKINNER. You haven't upset him? He's supposed to be giving an interview!

WINN. Upset *him?* He's upset *me!*

SKINNER. Writers! You can't take your eyes off them for a moment.

*Enter* DEEPING, *centre. He is enjoying himself.*

DEEPING. Very foolish to leave him up there on his own, you know, Winn.

WINN. Why? What's he doing now?

DEEPING. Listen.

*They listen. There is the noise of a large, heavy object falling down a flight of stairs.*

WINN. What in heaven's name . . .?

DEEPING. Your cabin trunk.

WINN. My cabin trunk?

*The noise of the object falling down another flight of stairs.*

DEEPING. He's bringing it downstairs for you.

WINN. Bringing it downstairs?

DEEPING. Ready for your departure.

*Enter* WALPOLE, *centre. Panting and gasping, beside himself with rage, he is dragging the cabin trunk. It is too heavy for him. He has a terrible struggle to get it through the door.*

WALPOLE. Never heard of such behaviour . . .!

WINN (*to* SKINNER). Look at him! Look! Look!

SKINNER. Calm down, Walpole.

WALPOLE (*drags trunk to middle of room*). Come back . . . soaked to the skin . . . whole morning utterly wasted . . .

WINN. Stop him! Stop him!

SKINNER (*to* WALPOLE). Now stop all this. You've got to be interviewed!

WALPOLE (*oblivious*). And what do I find? I find this little jackanapes . . .!

WINN. You've got to control him!

SKINNER (*to* WINN). Oh shut up! (*To* WALPOLE.) Control

yourself, Walpole!

WALPOLE. Now my heart's racing. Blood's pounding in my ears
. . . I won't remain in the same house! Either *he* goes, or *I* . . .

*Dies.*

SKINNER. That's better. Now listen, Walpole. This is going to
be just another ordinary, everyday literary interview. I don't
want you to go using this as an occasion for airing personal
grievances. All right, you may have grievances.

WALPOLE *slips out of sight behind the trunk.*

Fair enough — we all have grievances. We'll go into those at the
proper time . . . Where is he?

DEEPING. I think he's ill.

BLYTON. I think he's dead.

SKINNER. Oh, for goodness sake. Come on, Walpole, pull
yourself together. We've no time for this kind of thing now.
(*To* WINN *and* DEEPING.) Get him up. He can't sprawl about
the floor like that.

WINN *and* DEEPING *pull* WALPOLE *to his feet.*

Come on, Walpole! Work to be done!

*They sit him in a chair, then stand back to look at him.*

DEEPING. He doesn't look too good, you know.

WINN. I don't think he's really breathing.

SKINNER. He'll be all right. Just needs a bit of a sitdown. Get
his breath back.

WALPOLE *slowly keels forward.*

BLYTON. He's dead.

SKINNER. Of course he's not dead!

*Sits* WALPOLE *up again.*

DEEPING. It was heaving that trunk about that did it.

WINN. He always had a weak heart, I know that.

SKINNER. How are you feeling? A bit better?

WALPOLE *keels slowly forward again.*

BLYTON. He's dead.

SKINNER (*sits* WALPOLE *up again and holds him*). Well, we can't cancel the interview now.

DEEPING. He can't do an interview in this condition!

SKINNER. He's got to! He can't expect us to make more excuses at this stage! What would it look like? Be reasonable.

DEEPING. Well, if that Russian comes in and finds him like this . . . .

*Enter* KOCHETOV, *centre.*

KOCHETOV. Mr Walpole!

*They turn automatically to face* KOCHETOV. SKINNER *lets go of* WALPOLE, *who begins to keel forward.*

Please — don't get up!

SKINNER *pulls* WALPOLE *back.*

And don't say a word! Wait till my little girl from the Board of Trade comes in. She's just telling London we've found you.

*Crosses to centre door, and calls.*

WALPOLE *keels over.*

Trisha! Come on! He's here!

SKINNER *pulls* WALPOLE *up.* KOCHETOV *turns back to him.*

It's ridiculous! I thought you were dead!

WINN (*nervously*). No, no!

KOCHETOV (*turns to him*). I beg your pardon?

WALPOLE *keels over.*

WINN. No, no, no, no, no!

SKINNER *pulls* WALPOLE *up, and holds him.*

KOCHETOV. No, obviously not.

*Turns back to* WALPOLE, *glancing all the time at the centre door.*

KOCHETOV. If I might ask one thing of you. Trisha is very young, but she's very serious about it all, so — please — when she comes in, try not to smile.

*Enter* TRISHA, *centre.*

TRISHA. Is he really here?

KOCHETOV. He's really here! Mr Walpole, this is Trisha. Your greatest fan!

TRISHA (*shyly*). Hello.

*She looks at the floor. Silence.* KOCHETOV *watches her, amused.*

KOCHETOV (*to* TRISHA). Speak, then. Say something.

TRISHA. I don't know what to say.

KOCHETOV. Tell him you like his books.

*Pause.*

TRISHA. I can't say that.

KOCHETOV. Why ever not?

TRISHA. It just sounds silly.

KOCHETOV. Five hundred miles we have travelled for this moment. And not a word comes out!

TRISHA. Please just everyone go on with the conversation. Just forget about me.

KOCHETOV (*still looking at* TRISHA). She started reading your books when she was fifteen years old.

TRISHA. Mr Kochetov, please!

KOCHETOV. My love, *one* of us has to say something. She has three great heroes. Isn't that right? Tchaikovsky, Shelley, and Hugh Walpole.

TRISHA. I'll certainly never tell *you* anything again!

KOCHETOV. She's in love with all three of you. But you're a very lucky man, Mr Walpole, Because Tchaikovsky and Shelley — they're dead.

TRISHA. I hate you!

*Exit* TRISHA, *centre in tears.*

KOCHETOV. What have I done? But really, one can't help wanting to take a little bite out of her sometimes. Twenty years old, and she writes poetry still! I'll get her back, don't worry.

*Exit* KOCHETOV, *left.*

SKINNER (*panics*). Get him out of here!

WINN. But the interview . . .?

SKINNER. Out! Out! Out!

*Seizes* WALPOLE, *drags him out of his chair, and falls under the weight with* WALPOLE *on top of him.*

Off! Off! Off! Get him off! Help me!

WINN *and* DEEPING *lift him off* SKINNER.

DEEPING. Where shall we put him?

SKINNER. Anywhere! Outside! Not that way!

BLYTON. They'll be back any moment.

SKINNER. Just get rid of him!  Behind the sofa! In the box!

*Indicates the cabin trunk.*

DEEPING. In the box, right.

*Drops his half of* WALPOLE *and tries to open the trunk.* WINN *drops the other half and runs to defend the trunk.*

WINN. No, no! Not in there! That's my trunk!

SKINNER. It's locked! Where's the key?

WINN. Upstairs. You can't open it . . . Don't wrench it about like that! It's not made to be roughly handled . . .! Now look what you've done — you've broken it!

DEEPING. It's full of clobber.

SKINNER. Throw it out!

WINN. No, no! My things!

DEEPING *throws stuff out of the trunk.*

Look here, those are my tennis togs!

BLYTON (*at lefthand door*). He's coming!

WINN *abandons the defence of his property and scrambles with* DEEPING *and* SKINNER *to pick* WALPOLE *up off the floor. They dump him in the trunk (whence the actor playing him makes his escape via the stage trap, or any other means possible).*

DEEPING. Won't shut!

SKINNER. Foot!

*Points at a familiar galoshed foot which the jamming down of the lid has left sticking out.* WINN *and* DEEPING *cram it inside and close the lid.*

SKINNER *stands concealing the empty chair.*

*Enter* KOCHETOV, *centre.*

KOCHETOV. It's all right. I'm being unbelievably charming. She just needs to calm down and dry her eyes . . . First a trunk appears. Now a collection of old clothes.

*Picks up a handful of them.*

WINN. My tennis togs.

KOCHETOV. Won't the snow rather take the speed off the ball?

WINN. No, I'm just . . . sorting out my gear for next season.

KOCHETOV *tosses the tennis stuff aside and picks up another item. It turns out to be a pair of long johns.*

KOCHETOV. I'm sorry.

*He tactfully opens the trunk, and without looking throws the long johns into it.*

*Exit* KOCHETOV, *centre.*

DEEPING (*to* SKINNER). *Now* what?

SKINNER. Sit on the box!

WINN *sits.*

DEEPING. What are you going to tell them?

WINN. Tell them the truth.

DEEPING. Just suddenly . . .?

WINN. Just suddenly . . .

DEEPING. Got taken out and shot.

WINN. They can see he's not shot! They can see he just suddenly . . .

DEEPING. Dropped dead inside that box.

*Pause.*

SKINNER. That's where we went wrong — putting him in the box. Right. Get him out of there!

WINN. Take him out again?

SKINNER (*gestures to him to rise*). Up! Up! Up! Down!

*The righthand door is opening.* WINN *closes the lid and sits on it.*

*Enter* MCNAB, *right, without his apron, carrying the empty champagne bucket.*

DEEPING. Oh, it's you.

BLYTON. I thought it was Hugh Walpole's ghost.

*MCNAB crosses to the lefthand door with everyone staring at him. He stops, holds up the bucket and raps on its bottom to draw attention to the stamp.*

*Exit* MCNAB, *left.*

*WINN jumps up, and they start to lift* WALPOLE's *legs out of the trunk.*

SKINNER. Wait!

DEEPING. What?

SKINNER. McNab!

WINN. What about him?

SKINNER. Dress him up as Walpole! Say he's Walpole!

*Pause.*

BLYTON. Oh, *no!*

WINN. It would never work.

DEEPING. He doesn't look anything like him.

BLYTON. No, no. no!

WINN. It couldn't possibly work.

DEEPING. McNab's a Scotsman!

SKINNER (*indicates trunk*). The coat, the coat! Get his coat off! (*Calls off left.*) McNab! Come here! Where are you? McNab! (*To* BLYTON.) Keep that door shut! (*To* WINN *and* DEEPING.) Coat! Coat! Coat!

> DEEPING *shrugs. They open the trunk, and begin to remove* WALPOLE's *overcoat.*

> *Enter* MCNAB, *left, wearing an apron, carrying the empty champagne bucket and a garden fork.*

SKINNER. Right! Sit down! I've got a job for you.

> MCNAB *remains standing, looking into the trunk.*

MCNAB. What happened to *him*, then?

SKINNER. Nothing. Sit down.

MCNAB. Comes here first class. Goes home in the luggage van.

SKINNER. Sit down!

> *He takes the bucket and fork away from* MCNAB *and puts them on the sideboard.*

MCNAB. Sit down? (*Sits, in the chair previously occupied by* WALPOLE.)

DEEPING (*hands* SKINNER *the overcoat*). Hopeless! Hopeless!

SKINNER. Shut up!

DEEPING. It won't work!

SKINNER. It's got to work.

DEEPING. It can't work!

SKINNER. This is nothing! Inspections in factories — I've had men made out of *cardboard!* Flesh and blood — this is luxury! (*To* MCNAB.) Stand up!

> MCNAB *stands up.* SKINNER *and* WINN *dress him in the overcoat.*

Arms, arms, arms!

BLYTON. They're dressing him like a dummy!

SKINNER (*to* MCNAB). Listen, one foot wrong, and you'll be in that box along with him.

MCNAB. Hold fast now. What is all this?

WINN. You're him.

MCNAB. I'm what?

SKINNER. Don't argue, McNab. We've no time for argument.

WINN. You're Mr Walpole.

MCNAB. Mr Walpole?

WINN. Just for five minutes.

MCNAB. But why . . .?

SKINNER. Because I say you are.

WINN. What about the apron?

SKINNER. Keep the coat done up.

WINN. That neck's not Walpole.

SKINNER (*to* DEEPING). Muffler! (*To* WINN.) Get that cap off his head.

WINN (*removes cap and puts it in the pocket of overcoat*). Oh dear. Hugh's bald on top.

SKINNER. Hat!

DEEPING (*brings the hat*). Look at him, though! He's nothing like him!

SKINNER. Glasses! Two arms, two legs, and a head. That's enough for me.

DEEPING (*fetches the glasses*). He won't see much through these.

SKINNER. What does he need to see?

*They put the glasses on* MCNAB. *He feels around blindly.*

DEEPING. He must see where he's going.

SKINNER. He's not going anywhere. (*To* MCNAB.) Don't move. Don't wave your arms about.

DEEPING. But as soon as he opens his mouth . . .!

SKINNER. Don't open your mouth.

WINN. Be rather taciturn.

SKINNER. Just grunt.

WINN (*finds a pipe in overcoat pocket*). Here, chew this.

> *Pause. They stand back and survey their handiwork doubtfully.*

BLYTON. He only wants a bonfire under him.

> *Pause.*

WINN. He'll have to say *something*, Warden. If it's an interview.

MCNAB (*encumbered with the pipe*). Interview?

DEEPING. They always ask what your message for the world is.

WINN (*to* MCNAB). Your message for the world is the dignity of man.

DEEPING. He could tell them he's against war. That always goes down well.

BLYTON. What about love? They always ask about love.

SKINNER. You're for it. For love. Against war. Now, are we ready?

DEEPING. What does he think about Einstein? Or the Gold Standard? Or the League of Nations?

WINN (*to* MCNAB). Anything else — look at us. We'll help you.

SKINNER. Right. Are they coming?

> *Pause. They all wait, looking apprehensively at* MCNAB.

WINN (*to* MCNAB). Just . . . use your imagination.

> *Pause.*

SKINNER. Boots! Get his boots off!

> WINN *and* DEEPING *fall on a foot apiece and drag his boots off.*

WINN. No socks!

SKINNER. Boots back!

*They hurriedly replace the boots.*

*Pause.*

Box! Close the box!

WINN, DEEPING, *and* BLYTON *rush to the open trunk. They push the lid down, but it springs up again.*

WINN. It won't stay shut!

SKINNER. Sit on it!

DEEPING *sits on it.*

*Pause.* SKINNER *looks at* MCNAB.

It's not going to work, is it. Hopeless. Take all that stuff off. We'll just have to tell them the truth.

*Enter* KOCHETOV *and* TRISHA, *centre.*

TRISHA. I'm sorry. I don't know *what* you must be thinking.

SKINNER. Well, let me just explain.

TRISHA. I mean, a civil servant, bursting into tears and running out of the room like that.

KOCHETOV. It was my fault.

SKINNER. In fact it was Winn's fault.

TRISHA. It was everything. It was the train journey, and the feeling of being responsible for everything.

KOCHETOV. It was the snow. It was the sheep.

TRISHA (*to* MCNAB). It was finding you weren't here.

KOCHETOV. And then suddenly finding you *were.*

SKINNER. Yes, well, anyway . . .

DEEPING. Sit down, Skinner.

SKINNER. Oh. (*Sits.*)

TRISHA (*to* MCNAB). There are so many things I want to say to you — so many things I want to ask you about.

KOCHETOV. One look at you, and it all went out of her head.

TRISHA. Well, you were sitting here looking so — I don't know — so rigid and disapproving. I thought, well, he just despises me. But now I've had a proper look at you . . . well, you do look a bit less intimidating.

KOCHETOV. Now you've got your pipe to suck you're . . . well, you're an entirely different person.

TRISHA. Yes, you're not at all as I imagined you! I imagined you as . . . I'm not sure . . . (*Sits on the floor at his feet.*) But not wearing Wellington boots, somehow. Shall I tell you how I always think of you? It's very silly, but I always think of you as a cat. Awfully delicate and fastidious and feline, with beautiful manners and silky soft paws. But with piercing eyes that see right inside me! Well, that's how you look in your photograph. I suppose it doesn't show your feet. I'm sorry. I'm just babbling on. I don't know — I'm in such a funny mood today. First I can't start  and now I can't stop. (*To* KOCHETOV.) I'm sorry.

KOCHETOV. No — go ahead. Conduct the whole interview. Write the article for me.

TRISHA (*to* MCNAB). Well, I must ask you one thing. No, I mustn't. It's Mr Kochetov who's supposed to be asking the questions, and as a matter of fact I know what he's going to ask you, because he asks everyone we interview. He's going to ask you about the man in Nizhni Novgorod. (*To* KOCHETOV.) Sorry. Go on. Ask him about the man in Nizhni Novgorod.

KOCHETOV. You ask him. I'm sitting here having a holiday.

TRISHA. Don't be silly.

KOCHETOV. I'm not saying a word!

TRISHA. Well, apparently there's a man in Nizhini Novgorod who's sitting on top of a pole. Did you know there are people who sit on top of poles? This man's been up there for 83 days. (*To* KOCHETOV.) 83 days?

KOCHETOV. That was yesterday.

TRISHA. 84 days. And every morning newspaper reporters come

and stand at the bottom of the pole and ask the man what he thinks about war, and that kind of thing. And when Mr Kochetov was there, in Nizhni Novgorod, he asked him what the world looked like from the top of a pole, and the man replied . . .

KOCHETOV. 'Surprisingly large to be kept down by such a thin pole.'

TRISHA. And then Mr Kochetov asks you to say what the world looks like to you, in some brief and witty phrase like that. Well, I must stop talking, and let him ask you the question, but there's one thing I must just ask you first. Why is Isabel so strangely drawn to Moffatt's?

KOCHETOV. What?

TRISHA (to KOCHETOV). In Mr Walpole's novel, *Mr Perrin and Mr Traill*, which you haven't read. (*To* MCNAB.) She hates Moffatt's. So why does she keep coming back, again and again?

MCNAB *looks to* WINN *for help;* WINN *looks at* DEEPING, *who turns to* BLYTON. *She shrugs.* TRISHA *looks from one to the other.*

I'm sorry. Is that a very foolish question? (*To* MCNAB.) I'm sure everybody else knows. But please just tell me.

WINN. I know! Why don't we all have a drink?

DEEPING. A drink! What a good idea!

BLYTON. It's at least half-an-hour since breakfast.

WINN. A drink, Mr Kochetov?

KOCHETOV. If you like. (*To* MCNAB.) All right, let's get this question out of the way, and then we can do the interview. Tell her what Isabel is up to.

DEEPING. Just a moment. There's nothing to drink.

WINN. There's whisky.

BLYTON. He keeps it in his safe.

WINN. For special occasions.

DEEPING. Shall I do the honours, then?

> DEEPING *gets up from the trunk to cross to* SKINNER. *The lid opens.* BLYTON *gives a wild inarticulate cry.* WINN *hurls himself across to the trunk and sits on it.*

> KOCHETOV *and* TRISHA *turn to look at* BLYTON.

KOCHETOV. I beg your pardon?

BLYTON. Did I speak?

DEEPING (*holding out his hand to* SKINNER). I should think this is a special occasion, isn't it?

> SKINNER *gives him a key.*

> *Exit* DEEPING *centre.*

KOCHETOV. All right. Isabel. Set her mind at rest about Isabel.

WINN. I happen to know he's got rather strong views about war.

BLYTON. I want to hear him talking about love.

KOCHETOV. We shall come to war. We shall come to love. First, Isabel.

TRISHA. I'm sorry. I just wondered what the mysterious hold was that Moffatt's had over her.

> *She waits.* MCNAB *at last takes the pipe out of his mouth to reply.*

WINN. Or you could ask him if he's got a message for the world.

BLYTON. Or if he ever worries about who he really is.

TRISHA. Everyone keeps interrupting! No one's giving him a chance to speak!

KOCHETOV. Yes. Quiet, please, everyone. All right, this mysterious hold.

WINN. I think I should just explain . . .

KOCHETOV. Uh!

WINN. That he's a man of . . .

KOCHETOV. Please!

> *Silence.*

WINN. Very few words.

KOCHETOV. Then let us give him a chance to utter them. Mr Walpole . . .

*MCNAB removes his spectacles and rubs his eyes.*

SKINNER. What are you doing? (*To* KOCHETOV.) I beg your pardon. He has been strongly advised to keep his spectacles on at all times.

BLYTON. To reduce the chances of a sudden heart attack.

*MCNAB replaces his spectacles.*

WINN. They do take a close interest here in our welfare.

TRISHA. Please!

KOCHETOV. Let the man speak!

*MCNAB takes the pipe out of his mouth.*

*Enter* DEEPING, *centre, carrying a tray with whisky, soda and glasses.*

DEEPING. With soda or without soda?

*MCNAB puts the pipe back.*

TRISHA. He was just going to speak.

WINN. I'll be mother, shall I?

*Gets up from the trunk and crosses to the drinks tray. The lid of the trunk rises.*

SKINNER *utters a wild inarticulate cry.* KOCHETOV *and* TRISHA *turn to look at him as* DEEPING, *holding the soda syphon, hurls himself at the trunk.*

SKINNER *continues the cry as a cough.*

KOCHETOV *and* TRISHA *turn to look at* DEEPING, *who is sprawled across the trunk with the soda syphon spraying.*

DEEPING. Soda, anyone?

KOCHETOV. All right — who wants soda? I don't want soda. Anyone want soda? No one wants soda.

TRISHA. I want soda.

KOCHETOV. She wants soda.

*KOCHETOV takes her glass to* DEEPING *for a shot of soda.*

Now. Has everyone got a drink? Is everyone happy? No one wants to pass round the cigars, or run outside to wash their hands? All right. That's wonderful. We shall drink one toast together, and then we shall have absolute silence for Mr Walpole, while he explains to us all about the mysterious Isabel. So, ladies and gentlemen, may I ask you all to be upstanding . . .?

*Everyone gets to his feet except* DEEPING, *who is sitting on the trunk.* KOCHETOV *waits, glass raised, looking at* DEEPING. DEEPING *exhibits symptoms of stress. Then* BLYTON *jumps on to the trunk with raised glass.*

BLYTON. Isabel!

DEEPING *gets to his feet.*

OMNES. Isabel!

*They drink the toast and sit down —* DEEPING *and* WINN *on the trunk.* KOCHETOV *and* MCNAB, *still standing, take their drinks at one gulp.*

KOCHETOV. Oh, but look at *him!* He drinks like a Russian.

TRISHA. Now *you're* interrupting.

KOCHETOV. No, but this is a man after my own heart. Pour him another one. Pour me another one. We shall drink a toast together.

WINN *pours some more whisky for the two of them.*

SKINNER. Thank you. I think that bottle would be happier with me.

*Takes the bottle.* WINN *sits down on the trunk.*

KOCHETOV. To freedom of speech.

MCNAB *and* KOCHETOV *drain their glasses.*

And now, not another word from anyone. Mr Walpole . . .

KOCHETOV *sits down. A pause, then* MCNAB *leans forward a little in his chair.*

TRISHA. I think he really is going to speak!

BLYTON. And we all want to hear what on earth he's going to
say.

MCNAB. This fellow of yours . . . This fellow on the top of the
pole . . . Eighty-four days he's been up there? My word, he must
be bursting! Eighty-four minutes, this lot, and it's up with the
bedroom windy!

TRISHA. I don't understand . . .

KOCHETOV. Don't you, my love? I think perhaps I'm beginning
to . . .

*He gets out a notebook and pencil and begins to write.*

MCNAB. There's all of you below, looking up at him? Is that it?

*Gets to his feet and looks down at* KOCHETOV *and* TRISHA.

And there's him up above . . .

*He turns his chair round, and climbs on to it, as into a pulpit.*
SKINNER *hovers anxiously.*

. . . and he's been storing it up and storing it up, and now he
looks down and sees you at his feet, and what does he say? I'll
tell you what he says.

*He snatches the bottle of whisky from* SKINNER's *hand, and
holds it high above his head, tilted to pour. He puts his foot up
on the back of the chair, and his bare knee emerges from beneath
his coat.*

He says . . .

SKINNER (*screams*). Pull your skirt down!

Curtain.

## ACT TWO

*The same, with no lapse of time.*

SKINNER. Pull your skirt down!

MCNAB (*outraged*). My skirt? What do you mean, my skirt?

SKINNER. I mean, pull your trousers down!

MCNAB. Skirt, is it? (*Attempting to demonstrate to* TRISHA *and* MCNAB.) There's no skirt under here!

SKINNER (*trying to hold* MCNAB's *coat down*). Whatever will our visitors think?

WINN. They're short trousers.

DEEPING. His trousers are away for repair.

WINN. He's a Scoutmaster.

BLYTON. He is having treatment for this.

    MCNAB *hauls up his overcoat to demonstrate.*

MCNAB. It's the kilt!

SKINNER. It's not a kilt!

MCNAB. I'm a Scotsman!

SKINNER. He's not a Scotsman!

WINN. He is a bit Scotch.

DEEPING. More Scotch than most readers realise.

MCNAB. I'm a Scotsman!

SKINNER (*washes his hands of it*). All right — he's a Scotsman!

    *Pause.* SKINNER *goes and sits down, defeated.*

KOCHETOV (*to* TRISHA, *amused*). So — you weren't expecting a Scotsman?

TRISHA (*disconcerted*). He's not the sort of person I was expecting at all! (*To* MCNAB.) I thought from your books you'd be less . . . I don't know . . . (*To* KOCHETOV.) But didn't you?

KOCHETOV (*gravely*). Much less.

WINN. He is, he is.

TRISHA. You mean, less . . . ? (*She waves her hands, trying to capture the elusive quality she expected.*)

WINN. Oh, altogether less.

TRISHA. No, I mean I thought you'd be somehow more . . .

WINN. He is, in some ways.

BLYTON. Far, far more.

TRISHA. No, I mean more . . .

WINN. More fastidious.

TRISHA. Not exactly.

DEEPING. More spinsterly.

TRISHA. Well . . .

BLYTON. More feline.

MCNAB. Feline? Like a cat playing with a mouse? I can be feline.

KOCHETOV. You like watching people tie themselves into worse and worse knots? I understand that.

TRISHA. No, I know what I mean. I was expecting you to be much more Hugh Walpole-ish.

KOCHETOV (*to* DEEPING). Do you find him Hugh Walpole-ish enough?

DEEPING. Oh, he *can* be Hugh Walpole-ish, believe me!

BLYTON. My God, can he be Hugh Walpole-ish!

TRISHA. I don't think you're Hugh Walpole-ish at all!

KOCHETOV. I'm not sure what literary epithet springs to mind.

Rabelaisian, perhaps?

WINN. Well . . .

SKINNER. According to my records he is Episcopalian.

BLYTON. You should have seen him with the pilchards.

DEEPING. Oh, the pilchards, yes! He wasn't very Rabelaisian with the pilchards.

TRISHA. The pilchards?

MCNAB. Oh, don't talk to me about the pilchards!

KOCHETOV. And at once, of course, we talk to you about the pilchards.

MCNAB. Sunday dinner, it was. I've got them a tin of pilchards, and don't ask me where, because tins of pilchards don't grow on trees, believe me. So there all this lot sit, wolfing down their pilchards — except him.

TRISHA. Except whom?

WINN. (*indicates* MCNAB). Him.

MCNAB. Me?

WINN. You, Hugh.

MCNAB. What?

WINN. Hugh, you just sat there, Hugh. If you remember, Hugh.

SKINNER. Buck your ideas up, McNab . . . McWalpole . . .

MCNAB. Oh, yes. Right. Me it was that was sitting there. Right. So I just sat there, not eating, saying nothing, with a terrible pained expression on his face. On my face. So I said to him, 'What's the trouble, Mr Walpole?' I said to *me*, 'What's the trouble?' *He* said to me, 'What's the trouble?' He, the butler, said to me, Mr Walpole, 'What's the trouble?' And you know what I said? I said, 'I may be reduced to eating bread-and-butter without butter, and eggs and bacon without bacon or eggs, but I'll not eat pilchards without a fish-fork.'

DEEPING. You were always very punctilious about the silverware.

KOCHETOV. The perfect gentleman.

WINN. Exactly.

MCNAB. And the tea. He was forever on at me about the tea.
I was forever on at him about the tea. 'McNab,' I'd say, 'how
many times must I tell you? Tea in the teapot first. Milk in
the teapot afterwards. And McNab, don't pick up the sugar
with your fingers, or we'll have nothing but a teapotful of
germs.'

TRISHA. McNab? Who's McNab?

MCNAB. Oh, he's the butler. 'McNab,' I'm always saying to him,
'if you're the butler, then bustle about and buttle.'

DEEPING. 'McNab,' you'd say, 'don't stand there holding out
your greasy hand for the meal vouchers. Offer a tray.'

WINN. 'If you won't put on gloves to serve the residents, McNab,
at least take off the boots you've been wearing to serve the
pigs.'

MCNAB. I came in yesterday in a terrible state. You should have
seen my face as I walked through the door. It was a study.

*Crosses to righthand door to demonstrate.*

'It really is too bad. I came hideously close to doing myself a
mischief on the doorstep. But let people beware, McNab. I am
not entirely without cousins in certain quarters.' Oh, I'm quite
a character, I can tell you. I'm forever trying to get my hands
on ladies' underwear. 'McNab,' I say, 'have you heard any
whisper of knickers in the village? There's sixpence in it for
you, McNab. That rubbish they sell for men — I can't wear
it, McNab. It's too tickly for a man of sedentary disposition.'
(*Sits beside* KOCHETOV.) And the bathroom.

KOCHETOV. Tell us about the bathroom.

MCNAB. Every bath night the same. I come slopping down here
in my carpet slippers, and it's: 'McNab, here's sixpence for
you. Be a good lad and ventilate the bathroom for me. There's
somebody else's steam in there.' Carpet slippers — that's the
life. Some days I don't believe I get my feet out of those
carpet slippers from morning till night. Except when I'm up
there working, as they call it. I take my feet out of the
slippers, and I put them against the wall, just on the warm

patch where the kitchen flue comes through. I sit like that for hours together, and the dear knows what I'm thinking. Am I thinking up a few fine fancy notions to put in books? Or am I trying to remember from the old days whether you eat a grapefruit with a teaspoon or an eggspoon? I'll give you a word of advice, mister, and I'll give it you for nothing. When you get home, you buy yourself a good, hardwearing pair of carpet slippers, and you put up your plate as writer.

KOCHETOV. Today, I notice, you're wearing boots.

MCNAB. Today we've got company.

SKINNER. I hope our visitors are not taking all this too seriously.

KOCHETOV. I'm taking it very seriously. Almost as seriously as the rest of you.

WINN, DEEPING, *and* BLYTON *all hurriedly convert their anxious expressions into smiles.*

WINN. No, but he's a terrible tease, is Hugh. I'm sure that's not what he really feels about the writer's life.

KOCHETOV. Is it?

MCNAB. No, I'm pulling their legs. No, there's an awful lot of brain-fag attached to it. And then there's the strain on the eyes. And the spelling of some of those words is no joke. But, it's not without its compensations.

*Holds out his glass to* SKINNER, *who is forced to refill it.*

And see the rest of them are all right, will you. Keep them going with all those semi-colons and such.

SKINNER *fills the other glasses.*

No, looking back, over the years, taking the rough with the smooth, it's not a bad life. So here's to literature!

KOCHETOV. To literature!

TRISHA. Yes, to literature!

WINN
DEEPING } Literature!

SKINNER. Well, all good things must come to an end. So if

you've asked all your questions . . .

TRISHA. Oh, I don't think we have, have we?

KOCHETOV. On the contrary. We have hardly started.

MCNAB. No, I could tell you a thing or two about writers and what they get up to, never you fear. All that stuff about her heart beating wildly, and him pressing his burning lips against hers — I could tell you where they get that from, and it's not all out of books. Oh, my word, literature! Here's to it!

KOCHETOV. Literature — and life!

TRISHA. Life!

BLYTON. Life!

WINN
DEEPING } Literature.

SKINNER. And there we really must stop. I'm afraid Mr Walpole is a very busy man.

MCNAB. Don't worry about me, Mr Skinner. I've all the time in the world.

SKINNER (*genial*). Nose back to the grindstone, Walpole! Your readers are waiting!

MCNAB. Let them wait, Mr Skinner. Let everyone wait for once in a while.

SKINNER. (*to* KOCHETOV, *apologetically*). Writers! Half a chance, and they sit down and drink the day away. Come on, Walpole.

MCNAB. You want us all to get up and go back to work?

SKINNER. Yes. Up you get. (*To* KOCHETOV.) It's for their own good, I'm afraid.

MCNAB *rises.*

MCNAB. (*to* DEEPING, WINN *and* BLYTON). Right, then. Up we all get.

WINN. Oh . . .

*Looks anxiously at* SKINNER. DEEPING *looks at him sardonically. They remain sitting on the trunk.*

BLYTON. Perhaps we ought to sit and drink a little more of the day away first.

KOCHETOV. They can't bear to miss what's going to happen next.

SKINNER (*surrenders*). We're going to be here forever at this rate.

MCNAB *sits.*

TRISHA. Now you've taken off your glasses, I know where I've seen you before.

KOCHETOV. Here, when we arrived. With the pigfood.

MCNAB. Oh, the specs. Well, it's no use. I can't see a damn thing through them. They give you all these bits and pieces and say, 'Put them on.' And for all they care the floor can come up and hit you between the eyes.

TRISHA. And the apron.

MCNAB. Oh, the old apron.

SKINNER. He was cleaning his typewriter.

WINN. We were talking about how fastidious he is.

DEEPING. He is very fastidious about his typewriter.

TRISHA. But you had a bucket of pigswill.

DEEPING. His typewriter was in a disgusting state.

BLYTON. He drops bits of food into it as he types.

WINN. No, he was cleaning his room.

TRISHA. I see. You help with the jobs about the house?

MCNAB. You could say that.

DEEPING. We like to think of this place as a workers' co-operative.

WINN. We all share the domestic chores.

MCNAB. Oh, do we? (*To* TRISHA.) You ask him when was the last time *he* fed the pigs.

SKINNER. Well, we mustn't bore our visitors with our little

domestic arguments about who's done what.

MCNAB. Who's done what?

WINN. The usual family squabbles!

MCNAB. Who's done what? Who's done *any* what? What's *any* who done?

SKINNER. All right, the others remain seated — and you back to work . . .

MCNAB. I'll tell you who does what. I'll tell you who does *who*!

DEEPING *jumps up urgently.* KOCHETOV *smilingly makes a note.*

DEEPING (*to* KOCHETOV). A little more whisky? Oh, it's empty.

WINN (*jumps up*). I'll get another one.

*The lid of the trunk comes up.* WALPOLE's *legs become visible.*

SKINNER (*to* WINN). Look, I'm not standing for any more of this!

MCNAB. I should sit for it if I were you, Mr Skinner.

*He nods at the trunk.*

SKINNER. No, no, I'm not going to sit here and watch you open another . . .

*Sees the trunk. Sits down abruptly on it.* KOCHETOV *and* TRISHA *look round.*

SKINNER. . . . trunk of whisky.

WINN. Oh my God.

TRISHA. Are you all right?

MCNAB. His heart missed a beat.

DEEPING. He needs another trunk of whisky.

KOCHETOV. *Trunk* of whisky?

SKINNER. *Drunk* of whisky . . . What do I mean? Whusk of drunky.

DEEPING. Anyway, he needs one.

MCNAB. Come on, then, Mr Winn! It's the butler's day off.

DEEPING *gives* WINN *the key.*

WINN. No, all I meant was, we all make our own beds . . .

MCNAB. Bustle about and buttle, Mr Winn. That's your job for the day. Just buttle us another bottle.

*Exit* WINN, *centre.*

BLYTON. He'll have us all scrubbing the floors before this interview's out.

MCNAB. Don't you start. I know the kind of poems you write. 'Smouldering eyes and steaming thighs.'

BLYTON. You've been prying. You've been looking at my papers.

MCNAB. You left them on the bathroom floor.

BLYTON. And I did not write 'steaming thighs'.

MCNAB. You and that fellow that was here in November.

BLYTON. Dornford Yates? What about him?

MCNAB. In the billiard room. I saw the pair of you. Smouldering eyes, was it?

BLYTON. The expression to which I believe you're referring is 'slow-burning eyes'.

MCNAB. Slow-burning eyes in the billiard room. Steaming thighs in the gun room.

BLYTON. I have never set foot in the gun room. And I have never written any phrase remotely resembling 'steaming thighs'!

DEEPING. This is becoming intensely squalid.

BLYTON. Oh, thank you! Not as squalid as some things I could mention!

DEEPING. Oh, not that again. There is no truth in that story whatsoever. I scarcely knew the woman.

BLYTON. He scarcely knew her!

MCNAB. And he wasn't the only one who did!

SKINNER. Anyway, this sordid squabbling can hardly be of interest to our guests.

KOCHETOV. What? A real literary quarrel in front of our eyes? We're enjoying every moment of it! Aren't we, Trisha?

TRISHA. I must say, I do find it all . . . very surprising.

KOCHETOV. So fortunate we're here. You're all going to be the most famous writers in the world.

*Enter* WINN, *centre, with another bottle of whisky.*

SKINNER. Whisky! Give them some more whisky! Come on, come on!

DEEPING. Yes, let's all have another glass of whisky and change the subject.

WINN *refills their glasses.*

MCNAB. Who's done what? That's a good one. Who's cooked the breakfast? Who's cleaned Mr Skinner's boots?

TRISHA. But you don't do everything yourselves? You said there was a butler.

MCNAB. Oh, there's a butler right enough.

KOCHETOV. This is the unfortunate McDonald?

MCNAB. McNab. Capital m small c capital n. John McNab. The son of John McNab of Tomintoul. And John McNab of Tomintoul was the great-great-grandson of the famous John McNab of Craigellachie.

TRISHA. He was famous, was he?

MCNAB. He was famous enough in Craigellachie.

TRISHA. And where is this McNab today?

MCNAB. Ah! Now there's the question. Where is old McNab today? What's the answer to that one, then, Mr Skinner?

SKINNER. I don't think we need go into that.

MCNAB. (*to* KOCHETOV). I'll tell you where he is. He's . . .

SKINNER. (*sharply*). McNab! (*Realises.*) I mean . . . (*Calls.*) McNab!

WINN (*calls too, to help out*). McNab!

SKINNER. McNab!

WINN (*opens left-hand door, and calls off*). McNab . . . ! No, he's not there.

MCNAB. That's right. He's not there for once, and I'll tell you why — because for once he's . . .

SKINNER (*jumps to his feet authoritatively*). Drink! Another drink!

*The lid of the trunk rises.* MCNAB *calmly sits on it.*

MCNAB. . . . Because for once he's having a bit of a sit-down. (*Drains his glass and holds it out.*) I won't say no, Mr Skinner, I won't say no.

SKINNER *takes the bottle and refills* MCNAB's *glass.*

Yes, poor old McNab's having a bit of a sit-down. And I'll tell you something else. It's the first bit of a sit-down he's had today. In fact it's the first bit of a sit-down he's had since Hogmanay. And the only reason he had a bit of a sit-down at Hogmanay was that he found the key to the safe, and shortly after midnight, he still not having had a chance to get his backside to a chair, the chair upped and came for *him.*

SKINNER. Yes, and where was he for the whole of the next day?

MCNAB. In bed, a sick man!

KOCHETOV. You seem to be very concerned about this McNab fellow.

MCNAB. If I don't concern myself about him, none of this lot are going to.

SKINNER (*to* KOCHETOV). Please don't worry about the butler. He's well looked-after.

MCNAB (*to* KOCHETOV). Have you ever heard of a butler who gets the lunch?

SKINNER. Plenty of butlers get the lunch.

MCNAB (*to* KOCHETOV). Who goes *out* to get the lunch?

SKINNER. Plenty of butlers go out to get the things for lunch.

MCNAB (*to* KOCHETOV). From the snares he's set the night before? Have you ever heard of a butler who had to dig the garden and mow the lawns?

SKINNER. Those lawns haven't been mown since the pigs were let out on them.

MCNAB (*to* KOCHETOV). And tend the pigs? And repair the plumbing? And catch the rats? And shoot the poachers? And darn the socks? And then sit up all night hidden behind the chimney-stack with a pair of opera-glasses waiting to see who it is who's thieving the lead off the roof? And then come down in the morning and be accused of taking the lead himself? *And* the ping-pong ball! *And* the bucket for cooling the champagne!

SKINNER. I'm sure our visitors have seen far too much of the world to pay any attention to this nonsense.

MCNAB. 'Show me the pigswill, McNab'.

WINN. He has these dark moods.

MCNAB. 'McNab, I've stuck a tuppenny stamp on your bucket.'

BLYTON. They'll never stop him now.

WINN. Though we're all very fond of him. Aren't we?

MCNAB. You're all very fond of me today. You're right there. It's not like this every day of the week, mister, I can tell you. Even Mr Skinner's got a soft spot for me today. Isn't that right, Mr Skinner? Put your hand in the fire for me today, wouldn't you, Mr Skinner?

SKINNER. If there's anything I can do to help you, then naturally . . .

MCNAB. Jump to it fast enough if I asked you to jump, wouldn't you. Mr Skinner?

SKINNER. I don't know what all this is leading up to.

MCNAB (*quietly*). Jump, Mr Skinner. Let's see you jump.

KOCHETOV (*to* TRISHA). This is what happens when you put power into the hands of the people.

MCNAB. Jump.

SKINNER. I don't know what this is.

MCNAB. Jump.

SKINNER. I'm not playing games with you.

MCNAB (*gets up*). Jump!

> *The lid begins to rise.*

> SKINNER *springs to his feet in alarm.*

MCNAB (*sits*). Sit down.

> SKINNER *sits.*

> MCNAB *suddenly half-rises again — and again* SKINNER *rises, too. He at once sits down.* MCNAB *feints rising a third time — and still* SKINNER *cannot prevent himself jerking in response.*

> MCNAB *waves his hand dismissively, suddenly melancholy.*

> Sit down, sit down. You'll break our hearts.

KOCHETOV (*to* TRISHA). You see why we prefer autocracy.

> WINN *moves to sit down on the trunk beside* MCNAB.

WINN (*to* KOCHETOV). Oh, we do an awful lot of ragging at Balmoral. Don't we, Warry? A lot of apple-pie beds. A lot of drawing-pins on chairs.

DEEPING. Oh, we pull Blyton's pigtails. We pour treacle in Winn's socks.

KOCHETOV. It reminds me of War and Peace.

WINN. Really?

KOCHETOV. Prose fiction sustained to incredible lengths.

MCNAB (*gets up from the trunk and moves elsewhere*). Now, you asked how the world appeared to me.

WINN. Oh, no, I don't think so, Hugh. I don't think anyone asked you anything.

MCNAB. They asked me to describe the world as I would see it . . .

WINN. That was hours ago! That's all over now.

MCNAB. . . . As I would see it if I were sitting on the top of a pole.

BLYTON. He's going to go on all night.

MCNAB. Now, I'll be quite frank with you. To my eyes the picture is very black. Very black indeed. I look down from the top of my pole and what do I see? I see mistrust and suspicion between man and man. I see false accusation mounted upon a high horse, and slander raging. I name no names, but the people down there know who I'm looking at.

BLYTON. This is worse than his knees.

MCNAB. I see the drinking-cup chained to the fountain, and the stamp stuck to the bucket.

WINN, DEEPING, *and* BLYTON *are sunk in embarrassment.* SKINNER *gazes at* MCNAB *with defeated malevolence.*

I see lust in the billiard room and foreign silk undergarments in the gun room, and potatoes in the shops at ninepence a pound. And I stand up here on the top of my pole looking down at the world, and I hoist up my kilt, and I . . .

KOCHETOV (*smoothly, holding out his glass*). . . . pour us all another glass of whisky.

MCNAB *pours.*

Well, you did your best.

WINN. We did our best.

DEEPING. And we all got a glass of whisky out of it.

KOCHETOV. And it didn't work. The person I feel sorriest for is poor Trisha. Look at her! She's heartbroken!

TRISHA (*tries to smile*). No, no . . .

KOCHETOV. Five hundred miles we've come. The longest

journey she's ever made in her life. The first time she's ever been in a sleeping car. And all just to meet the great man, the famous writer. What did she expect to find?

TRISHA. I don't know what I expected to find.

KOCHETOV. But something. You hoped for something. A few words of wisdom.

TRISHA. No, not words of wisdom.

KOCHETOV. A little chat about books.

TRISHA. No, not books. I couldn't have talked about books.

KOCHETOV. Something in his face, then. Some special look that showed the pain and struggle inside. Something in his eyes. A little light from the fire within. A little warmth from the fire.

TRISHA. I can't remember now.

KOCHETOV. And what happens? First of all they won't let us see him. Then they won't let him speak. Then they make him talk a lot of nonsense about fish-knives. And in the end they can hide it no longer. A green apron — rubber boots — a passionate interest in the price of potatoes. Fish-knives! — The man's a peasant!

TRISHA. You think that's wonderful, don't you.

KOCHETOV. The most wonderful thing I've ever seen.

SKINNER. Heartbreaking, isn't it. You do your best, you make plans, you try to see your way through. And what happens? People let you down. You've got all the ideas — but you can't get the quality of people you need to carry them out. There just aren't the people.

KOCHETOV. My sweetheart, I'll tell you something about writers.

SKINNER. I could tell you a thing or two about people.

KOCHETOV. Writers are terrible people.

TRISHA. Some writers are, I'm sure.

KOCHETOV. All writers.

BLYTON. Some writers are terrible writers.

MCNAB. Some people are terrible people.

SKINNER. All people are terrible people.

KOCHETOV. Shall I tell you what writers talk about? One thing. Themselves. Oh, they tell you they hate war, of course. But is it war they care about? Not at all. What they care about is how they hate it.

TRISHA. You're just completely cynical.

KOCHETOV. Utterly cynical! Until today. Until I met Mr Walpole. Because, really, it's amazing. What Mr Walpole wants to talk about is not himself at all! It's another human being! What Hugh Walpole feels most strongly about is not Hugh Walpole — it's John McNab! An ordinary servant. A common butler. And yet, when Mr Walpole speaks about John McNab he becomes eloquent, he becomes passionate. He feels passionate resentment for McNab's wrongs. He feels passionate pride in McNab's ancestry. This — for me — is what the imaginative writer is seeking to do: to enter into the heart and mind of another. And when Walpole talks about McNab he *becomes* McNab! He *is* McNab!

TRISHA. I see what you mean. I suppose that is rather surprising.

MCNAB. The boots, was it, that gave it away?

KOCHETOV. Boots! Imagine! A writer in boots!

MCNAB. The thing about the boots is, they tried taking them off, but there was no socks.

KOCHETOV. No socks! My God! A writer with no socks! And you're ashamed of him! You even make him ashamed of himself! You don't deserve him!

SKINNER. Look, if I could just explain. McNab said that Walpole had . . .

WINN (*to* SKINNER). Have some more whisky.

SKINNER. I just want to explain . . .

DEEPING. Don't explain anything.

SKINNER. Yes, but it was all because McNab said . . .

DEEPING. Shut up!

SKINNER. What?

DEEPING. Listen to what he's saying, for heaven's sake!

WINN (*to* KOCHETOV). Please go on. A writer with no socks . . .

KOCHETOV. I must confess, I came to this country without faith. I came to mock. And I was wrong. I find that some things here really have changed. There are pigs in the palace gardens. A simple peasant can become a writer. I find here the possibility that society may after all be changed. That men may after all be transformed. Mr Walpole, I'm going to be very Russian for a moment. I hope you won't be embarrassed. I'm going to kiss you.

*Kisses* MCNAB *on both cheeks.*

MCNAB. Oh, my word! And I haven't shaved this morning!

TRISHA. Mr Kochetov — you've been converted!

KOCHETOV. Absurd! I'm the classic case! Came to mock and stayed to pray! And I can't tell you how ridiculously happy it makes me feel. As if some ancient heavy weight had been lifted off my heart.

TRISHA. Oh, Mr Kochetov! You're a different man!

*She kisses him.*

KOCHETOV. Volodya — call me Volodya.

TRISHA. Volodya! I thought you'd never see it!

KOCHETOV. I fought against it, Trisha! With all my force I struggled not to give in!

TRISHA. Volodya, I knew all the time you could do it if you tried.

KOCHETOV. It's Mr Walpole who did it. He's the one you should kiss.

TRISHA. Mr Walpole! I realise now I didn't understand you at all when I read your books. Or even when you were speaking. I feel as if *my* eyes had been opened, too.

*Kisses* MCNAB.

MCNAB. Oh, my word, literature!

TRISHA. I'm so happy!

KOCHETOV. You're so wise!

*Kisses her.*

MCNAB. Is this Wednesday? Or is it closing time?

KOCHETOV. So beautiful!

*Kisses* MCNAB.

TRISHA. So good!

MCNAB. Well, here's one for you, love.

*Kisses* TRISHA.

KOCHETOV. So new and strange!

*Embraces both of them together. They all laugh and kiss each other.*

SKINNER (*rises*). Perhaps I should just round the occasion off with a few words . . .

KOCHETOV (*ecstatic, ignoring* SKINNER, *his Russian intonation becoming rather more noticeable*). This is how it must be! No grass on the lawn — no socks on the feet! Only pigs and boots and sometimes a glass of spirits. This is how it must and shall be!

SKINNER. If I might break in here . . .

MCNAB (*raises glass*). To the pigs!

KOCHETOV. The pigs!

TRISHA. The pigs!

SKINNER. The pigs.

*They drink the toast.*

If I might just break in here. I should like, if I might, to propose a toast to the development of peaceful cultural relations between our two peoples . . .

KOCHETOV. To Hugh Walpole!

TRISHA. Yes, to Hugh Walpole!

SKINNER. All right, then, to Hugh Walpole.

MCNAB. To Hugh Walpole, the poor old devil.

*They drink the toast.*

KOCHETOV (*to* SKINNER). Isn't he wonderful?

SKINNER. Wonderful. So let me just say this before our guests depart. I believe that this has proved to be a most successful venture in promoting mutual understanding between our two great nations  . .

KOCHETOV. This other writer. He's another good writer. I can see it in his face. What's your name?

WINN. Winn. Godfrey Winn.

KOCHETOV. Godfrey. We drink to Godfrey.

OMNES. Godfrey!

*They drink.*

MCNAB. Speech!

KOCHETOV. Yes! Speech! Speech!

WINN (*rises*). Oh, Great Scott! I don't know what to say! Except to say oh my God!

*Sits down rapidly, to close the rising lid.*

*Cheers and applause.*

KOCHETOV. Wonderful! The perfect speech!

*Turns to* DEEPING.

And this writer here. Another fine writer.

WINN. Yes, here's to Warry!

OMNES. Warry!

*They drink.*

WINN. Speech!

KOCHETOV. Speech!

MCNAB. Come on, Mr Deeping!

DEEPING (*rises*). Well, that's very charming of you and I'm very touched. Because I should just like to say one thing. Today more than ever . . .

KOCHETOV (*jumps up*). Listen! Listen *I* make a speech!

*His accent has now become quite strongly Russian.*

KOCHETOV. Something I never tell before. Why did I hate England so much? Because I am half-English! Yes! My mother she was English. And when I am a child we are so poor, my mother and me!

DEEPING. Because today more than ever, we authors must fight for our rightful place . . .

KOCHETOV. Listen! Listen! So I think everything English it's poor and it's mean. As I grow up I think, English? I'm not English! I'm Russian! I'm like my father! But now I come to this country — now I come to this house — it makes me think again about my mother — and I see how hard life was for her . . . And that's all I want to say. What do you want to say?

DEEPING. All I want to say is this . . .

KOCHETOV. All I want to say is — I'm not Russian, I'm English.

*Cheers.*

DEEPING. Anyway . . .

KOCHETOV. So — wait — I understand all of you so well! Because, all of us, we have — in here — English soul!

SKINNER. Hear, hear.

KOCHETOV (*to* DEEPING). Now you make your speech.

DEEPING. Well, I only wanted to say one thing, and I've completely forgotten what it was.

*Cheers.* DEEPING *sits down, grinning.* KOCHETOV *turns to* SKINNER.

KOCHETOV. And then we have this man.

WINN. Yes, Mr Skinner! Arthur Skinner, isn't it?

KOCHETOV. Arthur Skinner. What can I say to you? You're a terrible man, Arthur !

SKINNER. Well, it's very kind of you to say so, but — I beg your pardon?

KOCHETOV. No. I must tell you frankly, Arthur — because we are speaking sincerely to each other now — we are speaking from the soul, yes? — I must tell you that you have many faults. No, wait. *Many* faults, and your worst fault is this: you are so humble. Wait! Wait! You are ashamed that everything in this house is so poor. You are ashamed that Hugh Walpole is a simple peasant. And you try to conceal these things from me.

SKINNER. No, no, no.

KOCHETOV. You tried to decieve me.

SKINNER. No, no, no.

KOCHETOV. Sincerely, Arthur. From all your soul.

SKINNER. Well . . .

KOCHETOV. Ah! 'Well.' You see? But, Arthur, let me tell you something. This poor house is a happy house. These simple people are happy people. And who is the head of this happy place? Arthur, let me tell you a surprising thing. The head of this happy place is you! (*Raises glass.*) Arthur Skinner!

OMNES. Arthur Skinner!

*They drink.*

SKINNER. I think that is the most wonderful thing that anyone has ever . . . I'm sorry . . .

MCNAB. Tears! From Skinner's eyes! This is like Moses smiting the rock!

SKINNER. No one has ever . . . I'm sorry . . .

KOCHETOV. Arthur, don't misunderstand! I'm not saying so very much!

SKINNER. I know. I know. But it just happens to be more than anyone else has ever . . .

KOCHETOV. Oh, Arthur!

MCNAB. Oh, now *he's* off!

KOCHETOV. I embrace you.

*Kisses* SKINNER *on both cheeks.*

SKINNER (*weeps openly*). Terrible . . . terrible . . . Haven't shed tears in all these terrible years . . .

TRISHA. Oh dear! You're making me cry!

*Holds* SKINNER*'s hand.*

MCNAB. This is as good as a funeral.

SKINNER. If my mother could be here now to hear you say what you said just then! When I think of all the struggles we had to make ends meet!

KOCHETOV. When I think of my mother with her safety-pins . . .

SKINNER. Scrimping and saving all week to make the books balance! Everything I know I learnt from her!

KOCHETOV. My mother the English governess. My father the count. And all these years I have tried to make myself like *him!*

*They weep.*

WINN. There's something about Russians. It just takes one Russian and a bottle of spirits, and in five minutes everyone's weeping!

KOCHETOV. English! I am Englishman!

WINN. One Englishman and a bottle of spirits. Well, I can't help thinking of *my* mother, and all the happy times . . .
Oh dear . . .

MCNAB. Go on, Mr Winn. Have a good cry. You'll feel all the better for it.

BLYTON. My God! If they could see what they looked like from here!

*They all turn and see her.*

DEEPING. Enid! We haven't toasted Enid!

BLYTON. Please don't worry about *me.*

WINN. We'd forgotten about you!

BLYTON. I'm quite used to being ignored.

SKINNER. Enid! Come here!

BLYTON. I've no wish to get involved in this public bathhouse of emotion.

*They absorb her into the group.*

KOCHETOV. You're a wonderful writer.

BLYTON. Oh, honestly . . .

WINN. No, she is, isn't she, Warry?

DEEPING. Wonderful!

KOCHETOV. And a very beautiful woman.

BLYTON. I just want to be left alone.

SKINNER. This is my house. No one's left alone in my house.

DEEPING. Let's give her a kiss.

*He and* KOCHETOV *kiss her.*

BLYTON. Oh, for God's sake . . .

SKINNER (*raises glass*). To Enid!

OMNES. Enid!

BLYTON. This is quite absurd.

KOCHETOV (*puts his arm round her*). But also quite delightful.

BLYTON. What's this thing? Oh God, it's a hand!

*She laughs. They all laugh.*

TRISHA. This is the best party I've been to for ages!

KOCHETOV. We cry. We laugh.

WINN. It's a Russian party.

KOCHETOV. English, English! I am Englishman!

DEEPING. Of course. It's an English party.

KOCHETOV. Soon probably we shall cry again. Because soon we shall be parted.

WINN. Never!

KOCHETOV. Who knows where fate will drive us? The earth is broad. Life is as vast and hazy as the autumn sky. Think of me sometimes!

SKINNER. I won't forget you! I can't remember your name . . .

KOCHETOV. Volodya.

SKINNER. Volodya.

KOCHETOV. Arthur . . .

SKINNER. Volodya!

KOCHETOV. Arthur . . . Arthur . . .

*Feels in his pockets.*

I want to give you something -- something of mine — so you remember me, Arthur . . . This watch. Take this watch, Arthur.

SKINNER. Volodya, it's gold!

KOCHETOV. It's nothing.

SKINNER. It's got fourteen jewels!

KOCHETOV. It's yours. Trisha . . . Godfrey . . .

*He begins to distribute the contents of his pockets to everyone.*

I want you all to have something . . .

TRISHA. But these are your cigars.

KOCHETOV. Take them, take them.

WINN. But you'll need your fountain pen!

KOCHETOV. I need nothing, Godfrey.

SKINNER. Volodya — it's got a second hand!

DEEPING. I can't accept money.

BLYTON. No, no, no — not money.

KOCHETOV. Money — it's dirt.

DEEPING. But this is thirty-five pounds!

BLYTON. This is four and ninepence-halfpenny!

MCNAB. What's this? His pocket comb?

WINN. It's like Christmas!

SKINNER. Volodya — it's got luminous numbers!

*But* KOCHETOV *is busy tearing off his jacket and tie and distributing them.*

KOCHETOV. Here . . .! Here . . .! Why should I have all this? I am rich. You are poor.

TRISHA. No, no, no!

DEEPING. No more!

WINN. You must keep your trousers!

*They all restrain him by force.*

DEEPING. How can we ever repay you as it is?

TRISHA. I can't think of anything except this brooch.

WINN. Look, this is a clean handkerchief.

MCNAB (*gives him* WALPOLE's *hat*). Try this hat.

BLYTON. And this scarf.

DEEPING. I want you to have this picture of my mother.

SKINNER. One and twopence — it's all I've got on me.

KOCHETOV. Oh, but this is lovely . . . this is beautiful . . . I shall keep this always.

SKINNER (*holds up his hands for silence*). Listen! I should just like to say, with all my heart . . . I don't know what I'd like to say!

BLYTON. I know! We must swear that we'll always be friends!

KOCHETOV. We swear a solemn oath!

BLYTON. We'll be a kind of gang!

TRISHA. Yes!

BLYTON. And it'll be a secret! We'll be the Secret Seven!

OMNES. The Secret Seven!

KOCHETOV. We put our hands on our souls.

WINN. Where are our souls?

KOCHETOV. Here. (*The heart.*)

SKINNER. And we swear!

BLYTON. To be friends for ever and ever and ever!

KOCHETOV. And never to deceive each other again!

BLYTON. Never!

SKINNER. Never!

KOCHETOV. And also never to forget . . .

*He stops. A thought has struck him. They all stand, hand on heart.*

WINN. Never to forget what, Volodya?

KOCHETOV. John McNab!

WINN. John McNab?

KOCHETOV. Your wonderful butler! He must come and swear with us! Where is he?

TRISHA. Yes! Where is he?

WINN. Oh . . .

DEEPING. Well . . .

WINN (*takes his hand away from his heart*). He's lying down.

KOCHETOV. Bring him in.

DEEPING. He's out for a walk.

KOCHETOV. Lying down? Out for a walk?

MCNAB. He doesn't know where he is, and that's the truth.

KOCHETOV. Why are you saying these things to me? We swore! Arthur, we swore!

SKINNER. We did. We swore, Godfrey! We swore, Warwick! (*Starts to laugh.*) And, Volodya, it's so ridiculous! You're never going to believe it!

KOCHETOV. What?

TRISHA. What?

SKINNER. McNab's here! Right in front of your eyes.

WINN. Arthur!

DEEPING. Moderation in all things!

BLYTON. Don't spoil everything when it's all so nice!

SKINNER. He'll understand! We don't have to have secrets any more! He's not that kind of person!

KOCHETOV. You mean . . . one of these people is . . .?

SKINNER. You're going to be so cross!

WINN. Arthur, *please* . . .!

KOCHETOV (*indicates* WINN). You're not saying *he* is . . .?

SKINNER. No!

DEEPING. He's gone mad!

KOCHETOV (*indicates* DEEPING). You mean *him?*

SKINNER. No!

KOCHETOV (*turns to* BLYTON). Not *her?*

SKINNER. No! So that only leaves . . .? Oh, Volodya, you're going to kick yourself!

> KOCHETOV *and* TRISHA *slowly turn towards* MCNAB *and gaze at him.*

KOCHETOV. You're not trying to tell me . . .?

MCNAB. Oh, and it was a good coat, too.

> *Resignedly takes off* WALPOLE's *overcoat.*

WINN. Arthur, you can't start saying that Hugh Walpole is McNab.

BLYTON. Because where would Hugh Walpole be in that case?

SKINNER. In what case?

DEEPING (*opens the trunk*). In *that* case!

KOCHETOV. You mean it's . . .?

SKINNER. Not him.

KOCHETOV. *Not* him?

TRISHA. But there's no one else in the room! Except you.

DEEPING. She's guessed it!

WINN. Brilliant!

KOCHETOV. *He's* McNab?

BLYTON. Obvious as soon as you think about it.

KOCHETOV. *You're* McNab?

SKINNER. I'm McNab.

MCNAB. He's the butler, is he? Well, I'll not be the one to argue with him.

KOCHETOV. I don't believe it.

MCNAB (*takes off the green baize apron*). Here — put on the apron. We'll soon see. Where's the cap . . .?

*Gets it out of the pocket of* WALPOLE's *overcoat.*

Put this on, McNab, or you'll be catching your death out there in the piggeries . . . There he is! There's your butler!

*They all gaze at* SKINNER, *as he stands amongst them in flat cap and apron.*

KOCHETOV. I don't believe it. I don't believe it! *I don't believe it!*

*But it is clear from his delighted tone that he does.*

MCNAB *refills his own glass.*

MCNAB. John McNab!

*Everyone snatches up a glass to toast* SKINNER.

OMNES. John McNab!

MCNAB. May he increase and multiply!

*They drink the toast.* KOCHETOV *embraces* SKINNER.

KOCHETOV. But really, it's amazing! I was completely deceived! Weren't you, Trisha? I believed absolutely and entirely that you were Arthur Skinner! So you're John McNab.

SKINNER, *still in a state of shock after his error, does his best to smile and nod.*

The perfect butler. The man who does everything.

SKINNER *smiles and nods.*

Even makes a fool of visiting journalists. Oh, John, John, John! May I call you John?

SKINNER *smiles and nods.*

Of course, I really knew it all the time. You were making this man so exaggerated! The books — the kedgeree — the pig food. All the time I just wanted to laugh!

SKINNER. Yes, well, all right, it may seem funny to you. But *someone's* got to worry about the books. *Someone's* got to sort out the kedgeree from the pigswill.

KOCHETOV (*to the others*). Listen to him! He understands this man's type exactly!

SKINNER. You don't think he *wants* to be that type, do you? He hates it! He'd rather be one of this lot, and sit around writing books all day. He'd rather be McNab, even!

KOCHETOV. He envies you?

SKINNER. What? Me? (*Sees the green baize apron he is wearing.*) Yes! Me! He'd rather be me!

MCNAB. That's a new one.

SKINNER. He would! He would! Of course he would! No responsibilities. No worries. Nothing to do but slollop around the house all day with a bucket of pigswill. There's even something about the way I hold the bucket that gets on Skinner's nerves.

KOCHETOV. Why? How do you hold it?

SKINNER. Where is it?

MCNAB *fetches the champagne bucket and fork from the sideboard and hands them to* SKINNER.

Nothing to do but play with buckets and spades and make poor Skinner's life a misery. It's as good as being back at school!

MCNAB. Off you go then, McNab, and muck out the piggeries.

SKINNER. I come in that door . . . (*Imitates* MCNAB.) Never think of putting the bucket down to close it. Oh no. Always put my leg up behind me, like a dog at a lamp-post, and kick it with my filthy boot. Then off I go, swinging the bucket about, swaggering around as if I owned the place. I've got a way of moving my shoulders somehow — it's a calculated insult.

DEEPING, WINN, *and* BLYTON *laugh and applaud.*

MCNAB. What's this?

WINN. This is you!

KOCHETOV. This is *him?* (*Indicates* MCNAB.)

WINN . I mean, it's *him.* (*Indicates* SKINNER.)

DEEPING . He's got himself exactly.

MCNAB (*amused in spite of himself*). He never prances around like that.

WINN )
DEEPING }   He does! He does!
BLYTON )

SKINNER. Every syllable I utter is a studied mockery. (*Imitates* MCNAB.) Fair enough, Mr Skinner. It's only a bucket of kedgeree, Mr Skinner. And it's yes, Mr Skinner, and no, Mr Skinner, and three buckets full, Mr Skinner, and never taking a blind bit of notice all the same.

MCNAB (*delighted*). Oh, but he's got the trick of it now, hasn't he.

KOCHETOV. And you're a Scotsman all the time!

SKINNER. Oh, by God, am I a Scotsman!

KOCHETOV. I knew that English accent wasn't real!

SKINNER. Oh, it's whishty-tushty, Mr Skinner. It's Dundee and Dundoon. It's crallochs and bollochs and wee cowerin' beasties.

MCNAB. What language is this?

SKINNER. I'm a Scotsman, right enough. As pig-headed as granite. As lofty as a mountain. As prickly as that pair of antlers. But not above snitching up anything that's left around. Oh no!

*He slyly finishes up a glass of whisky in passing.*

Not too proud to poke my wee snoutie into what dusnae concern me.

*Slyly opens in passing the file that contains* DEEPING's *work.*

MCNAB (*delighted*). Oh, but isn't he the fellow!

SKINNER. Oh, I'm the fellow today! When I've got the old accent on! When I've got the old green baize apron round me! There's no holding me now!

*Crosses towards righthand door.*

Oh, it's a sly wee cowerin' creature I am! And all the time, right under poor wee Skinner's nose, it's . . .

*He stops dead. His accent returns abruptly to English as he realises.*

Green baize aprons!

KOCHETOV. What? What?

SKINNER. Every time I go out I've got it on. Every time I come back I haven't.

*He turns accusingly upon* MCNAB.

Green baize aprons! That's what I'm stealing!

MCNAB. Oh, there's no fooling him today!

DEEPING. Of course!

WINN. Of course!

BLYTON. But that's beautiful!

KOCHETOV. You steal, do you, McNab?

SKINNER (*looking at the apron in amazement*). Two dozen, there were. And out they went, right in front of Skinner's eyes!

KOCHETOV (*to* TRISHA). What a character!

SKINNER. That's it! That's his life! Aprons and lavatory chains. Buckets and ping-pong balls. And there it goes . . .

*He follows the imaginary progress of the aprons from lefthand door to righthand.*

Out of the front door and away! And listen! Listen!

*He jumps on to the trunk.*

I just want to say that this is the happiest day of my life! Two hours ago we were all so worried! What were we worried about?

*Three dull thuds, off. All of them except* KOCHETOV *and* TRISHA *freeze.*

KOCHETOV. What? What?

TRISHA. Someone at the door . . .

BLYTON (*sombrely*). That's what we were worried about.

KOCHETOV. Someone at the door?

MCNAB. The Inspector.

KOCHETOV. What inspector?

SKINNER. The Government Inspector.

*Three more dull thuds, off.*

KOCHETOV. The Government Inspector? He comes here? But this is wonderful! He sees this happy house — he gives everyone a medal! Let him in!

SKINNER (*dubiously*). Let him in!

KOCHETOV. Don't worry! Leave it to me! I tell him everything! How happy we are! The Secret Seven! Everything!

BLYTON (*moved*). Oh, Volodya! We could be married! I could write children's books! I've always wanted to write for children!

KOCHETOV (*to* SKINNER). Let him in!

DEEPING, WINN,
BLYTON, MCNAB,      (*to* SKINNER, *happily*). Let him in!
TRISHA

SKINNER *is just about to get off the trunk.*

KOCHETOV. Wait!

*He quickly picks up the empty whisky bottles.*

Even in paradise . . .

SKINNER *jumps down from the trunk and goes out, right. The others all turn in the same direction as* KOCHETOV *opens the trunk.*

. . . dead men to hide!

*He puts the bottles inside the trunk, closes the lid and sits on it, then realises what he has seen, just as the others realise what he has said and turn back to look at him.*

*Curtain.*

Further titles in the Methuen Modern Plays
are described on the following pages.

## Methuen's Modern Plays

| | |
|---|---|
| Barrie Keeffe | *Gimme Shelter (Gem, Gotcha, Getaway)* |
| | *Barbarians (Killing Time, Abide With Me, In the City)* |
| | *A Mad World, My Masters* |
| Arthur Kopit | *Indians* |
| | *Wings* |
| Larry Kramer | *The Normal Heart* |
| John McGrath | *The Cheviot, the Stag and the Black, Black Oil* |
| David Mamet | *Glengarry Glen Ross* |
| | *American Buffalo* |
| David Mercer | *After Haggerty* |
| | *Cousin Vladimir* and *Shooting the Chandelier* |
| | *Duck Song* |
| | *The Monster of Karlovy Vary* and *Then and Now* |
| | *No Limits To Love* |
| Arthur Miller | *The American Clock* |
| | *The Archbishop's Ceiling* |
| | *Two-Way Mirror* |
| | *Danger: Memory!* |
| Percy Mtwa<br>Mbongeni Ngema<br>Barney Simon | *Woza Albert!* |
| Peter Nichols | *Passion Play* |
| | *Poppy* |
| Joe Orton | *Loot* |
| | *What the Butler Saw* |
| | *Funeral Games* and *The Good and Faithful Servant* |
| | *Entertaining Mr Sloane* |
| | *Up Against It* |
| Louise Page | *Golden Girls* |
| Harold Pinter | *The Birthday Party* |
| | *The Room* and *The Dumb Waiter* |
| | *The Caretaker* |
| | *A Slight Ache and other plays* |
| | *The Collection* and *The Lover* |

John Kirkmorris: *Coxcombe;* John
Peacock: *Attard in Retirement;* Olwen
Wymark: *The Child*)

*Best Radio Plays of 1981* (Peter Barnes:
*The Jumping Mimuses of Byzantium;*
Don Haworth: *Talk of Love and War;*
Harold Pinter: *Family Voices;* David
Pownall: *Beef;* J P Rooney: *The Dead
Image;* Paul Thain: *The Biggest
Sandcastle in the World*)

*Best Radio Plays of 1982* (Rhys
Adrian: *Watching the Plays Together;*
John Arden: *The Old Man Sleeps
Alone;* Harry Barton: *Hoopoe Day;*
Donald Chapman: *Invisible Writing;*
Tom Stoppard: *The Dog It Was
That Died;* William Trevor: *Autumn
Sunshine*)

*Best Radio Plays of 1983* (Wally K Daly:
*Time Slip;* Shirley Gee: *Never in My
Lifetime;* Gerry Jones: *The Angels They
Grow Lonely;* Steve May: *No
Exceptions;* Martyn Read: *Scouting for
Boys*)

*Best Radio Plays of 1984* (Stephen
Dunstone: *Who Is Sylvia?;* Don
Haworth: *Daybreak;* Robert Ferguson:
*Transfigured Night;* Caryl Phillips:
*The Wasted Years;* Christopher Russell:
*Swimmer;* Rose Tremain: *Temporary
Shelter*)

*Best Radio Plays of 1985* (Rhys
Adrian: *Outpatient;* Barry
Collins: *King Canute;* Martin
Crimp: *The Attempted Acts;*
David Pownall: *Ploughboy
Monday;* James Saunders:
*Menocchio;* Michael Wall:
*Hiroshima: The Movie*)